THE BOXERS OF WALES

OF WALES

Volume 5: Newport, the Gwent Valleys and Monmouthshire

GARETH JONES

ST DAVID'S PRESS

Cardiff

Published in Wales by St. David's Press, an imprint of

Ashley Drake Publishing Ltd
PO Box 733
Cardiff
CF14 7ZY

www.st-davids-press.wales

First Impression – 2017

ISBN 978-1-902719-63-4

© Ashley Drake Publishing Ltd 2017
Text © Gareth Jones 2017

British Library Cataloguing-in-Publication Data.
A CIP catalogue for this book is available from the British Library.

Typeset by Replika Press, India
Printed by Akcent Media, Czech Republic

Contents

Two Gwent boxers were chosen as reserves to the 1952 British Olympic squad: Parry Dando, from Llanhilleth, and Richie Jenkins, of Griffithstown (front row, second and third from left) pose with team-mates including two Welshmen, Dai Dower (middle row, far left) and Terry Gooding (back row, fifth from right, next to Henry Cooper).

ACKNOWLEDGEMENTS

This volume may have one name on the cover, but there are dozens of others who have played vital roles in its production.

First and foremost come the boxers, past and present, without whose courage and skill there would have been nothing to write about. But the contributions of those still with us have gone beyond that. They have been, without exception, generous with their time and patience.

In writing about those gone before I am indebted, not merely to the often anonymous reporters who attended their fights, but to the families and friends who have helped me put flesh on the bones of a bare statistical record.

But there are many others, unconnected with the boxers profiled, who have assisted my research. Among them are the editors, past and present, of *Boxing News*, Rob Smith, of the British Boxing Board of Control, and the secretary of its Welsh Area Council, Mark Warner. John Waith and Alasdair McIntyre, of the Welsh Amateur Boxing Association, and Cyril Thomas, from the Welsh Ex-Boxers' Association, have also played their parts.

People at other organisations, separate from the sport, have made a labour of love even more enjoyable. I refer particularly to the helpful staff at Cardiff and Newport libraries and the Gwent Archives in Ebbw Vale, as well as the co-ordinators and members of numerous local history societies and their websites.

There are many individuals, too, who deserve a name check, among them Wynford Jones, Dave Furnish, Patrick White, Andrew Penman and Alex Daley.

Most of the photographs included have been loaned by the fighters, their families and some of those mentioned above. But I am especially grateful to the *South Wales Argus* and hard-pressed professionals who have allowed me to use their work, including the Huw Evans Picture Agency (www.huwevansimages.com), Peter Westall, Jane Warburton, Jon Scriven, Ciaran Gibbons and Kris Agland.

Thanks, too, to my publisher, Ashley Drake, for his unwavering support. And, as always, to Harold Alderman, MBE, whose willingness to share the results of his years of research has saved lesser historians like myself countless hours of toil.

FOREWORD

If someone asks me where my love of boxing comes from, I think of a pair of battered old gloves which used to hang in my grampa's shed. Whenever we kids got bored on a summer afternoon, he would pull them on and stage an exhibition for us. In between he would tell stories of his days on the booths and of the exploits of fighters like Johnny Basham, Percy Jones and Gipsy Daniels. Those tales have stayed with me throughout my life.

For so many miners in the valleys, life was hard and the extra pennies my grampa earned on the booths ensured there was food on the table for his eight children. Perhaps, had he not been injured in the pit, I like to think someone might have chronicled his career.

Growing up in the eighties, I can remember the excitement when Newport boxer David Pearce won the British heavyweight title. Suddenly it seemed possible that the world heavyweight king could be a Welshman – and from Gwent as well!

Dreams of a world champion from the county were to become a reality in the 1990s. Bantamweight Robbie Regan claimed a belt in 1996 and the following year saw the start of Joe Calzaghe's decade-long reign.

It wasn't just the fighters who were making their mark either. The other famous Calzaghe, Joe's father Enzo, once had three world champions in his gym. More recently, Gwent boasted a double world champion in the shape of Cefn Fforest's Nathan Cleverly.

When you think about it, it's amazing how this small part of Wales has managed to place itself at the heart of British boxing. These pages tell the remarkable stories of the men who made it happen.

Christopher Evans
Member of Parliament, Islwyn

INTRODUCTION

The fighting tradition of the old county of Monmouthshire is both long-lived and fruitful. And, for all the professional curmudgeons who insist our sport is on its last legs, the last few decades have been the most glorious.

The area has produced no fewer than four world champions since 1996. Robbie Regan was quickly followed by Joe Calzaghe. Gavin Rees added a second crown for Newbridge and, more recently, Nathan Cleverly joined them.

The local enthusiasm for boxing was particularly evident during World War II. While most of Britain was starved of entertainment, the scene was still buzzing in the Gwent valleys. Booth owner Joe Gess, in Pontypool, and publican Jack Matthews and his partner, Albert Evans, in Crumlin, defied the blackout, transport problems and the rest to provide regular shows for the eager punters.

In an earlier era, prizefighting was frequently an added attraction to horse racing and one of the earliest recorded examples in the county saw 4,000 people at an 1824 meeting in Monmouth look on as a quarryman named Parry beat a rival called Powell over 103 rounds.

Many big names dropped by, making public appearances before huge crowds. Tom Sayers stayed at the Angel Hotel, Monmouth, in 1861, a year after his legendary set-to with American John Camel Heenan. He caused the biggest stir in the town since Lord Nelson turned up with his mistress, Lady Hamilton, and her elderly husband. And Heenan, the 'Benicia Boy' himself, also called in while touring with a circus.

Sayers also visited Newport, while former world heavyweight champion Tommy Burns displayed his skills at Chepstow in 1921, more than a dozen years after he was dethroned by Jack Johnson. Most famously, the reigning holder of the "Greatest Prize in Sport", Joe Louis, boxed an exhibition at Newport Athletic Ground on June 30, 1944. Another world champion, former feather king Jackie Wilson, acted as referee.

This volume is intended as a tribute to all those, champions and journeymen, inside and outside the ropes, who have played their part in the area's fistic history.

Gareth Jones
September 2017

ROY AGLAND
(1926-2006)

🏴 Welsh Middleweight Champion 1952-55

Aworkman is only as good as his tools, they say. The southpaw from Tiryberth was an excellent workman, but his tools let him down. Synovitis in his hands wrecked his hopes of competing in the Olympics and then forced him into retirement when on the brink of a British title shot.

A boxer from childhood, Roy Agland won the British ABA middle tournament in 1947, seeing off soldier Ron Bebbington in the final despite boxing on one good leg, and was promptly selected for the European championships in Dublin a fortnight later. Unfortunately, the ankle damaged at Wembley meant no trip to Ireland.

And, with the London Olympics looming, persistent hand problems ruled the 21-year-old steelworks shunter out of the 1948 Welsh championships and therefore the chance to defend his British ABA crown. Despite that setback, he was named as reserve to the new champion, Seaman Johnny Wright.

Wright went all the way to the final, where he became the victim of Hungarian legend Laszlo Papp, winning the first of his three Olympic golds. Who knows what Agland might have achieved?

It was late 1950 before Roy finally dipped his toes in the pro ring, but father-trainer Glyn found it difficult to attract opponents. Roy had been idle for 18 months before he took on unbeaten fellow-lefty Jimmy Roberts at Abergavenny and dazzled in handing the Newbridge man his first defeat, reproducing the all-round skills that had brought him such success in the amateur ring.

Not everyone was impressed, however. The Welsh Area Council decided to ignore events at the Market Hall and nominated Roberts to challenge newly crowned

Roy Agland

Welsh middleweight champion Ron Cooper. But when Roberts dethroned the Pyle man Agland was called up to be his first rival.

The pair returned to Abergavenny on December 1, 1952, for the title shot. The taller Tiryberth fighter was able to catch Roberts marching in, but the champion absorbed the punches and scored regularly himself with two-handed attacks until the second half of the bout. Then it became clear that Agland's power had weakened Jimmy and, as the 10th round began, a right hook sent him to the floor.

When he rose, Roy drove him around the ring before keeping him in a corner as he unloaded his artillery. Eventually, the champion slid down the ropes to the canvas and, despite an effort to rise at eight, collapsed again to take the full count. He was taken to hospital afterwards, still unconscious; although he recovered during the night, he never boxed again.

Plans to tempt former world champion Randy Turpin into a British title defence came an almighty cropper at the first hurdle. Wally Beckett, from Carshalton, interrupted his honeymoon to turn up at Sophia Gardens Pavilion and knocked Roy out in 72 seconds. It was the Welshman's own fault. The referee had halted the action to speak to Beckett for a minor infraction and Agland dropped his gloves to his sides; when ordered to "Box on!" he was too slow to prevent a right to the jaw dropping him to a sitting position and he was counted out, draped across the bottom rope.

There would be no repeat of such carelessness. A visit to Liverpool saw him stop Belfastman Tom Johnston – ending his career – and when conqueror Beckett was tempted back to Sophia Gardens he was kept firmly on the end of Roy's right lead and comfortably outpointed.

Many Welsh fans thought Agland lucky to get verdicts over flashy Trinidadian Hector Constance and Yorkshireman George Dilks, but the knowledgeable patrons at Liverpool Stadium were mightily impressed when he turned up to outclass local banger Billy Ellaway. It seemed that Roy had rediscovered his form. In fact, it was his last hurrah.

The hand trouble had become too bad to ignore. There were suggestions of a comeback, but it never happened. For a while Agland ran a pub at Fleur-de-Lys before moving to Cardiff and taking over the Roath Youth amateur club formerly guided by his father-in-law, the legendary Bill Mannings, and becoming a top trainer himself.

And while he may have missed out on the London Olympics as a competitor, he made it to Moscow in 1980 as one of the coaches on the British team.

Ten-year-old Roy keeps his hands up

JAMIE ARTHUR
(1979-)

- 🥊 **Commonwealth Super-Bantamweight Champion 2010-11**

- 🥊 **British Featherweight Challenger 2010**

- 🥊 **British Super-Bantamweight Challenger 2011, 2012**

- 🥊 **Welsh Super-Featherweight Champion 2009-10**

- 🥊 **Commonwealth Games Gold Medallist 2002**

Delight was mixed with surprise as Welsh fight fans listened to *Hen Wlad fy Nhadau* ring out for only the third time in the history of Commonwealth Games boxing.

There had been optimism that the red dragon might be hoisted to signal a successor to pre-war star Denis Reardon and the revered Howard Winstone, triumphant on home ground in Cardiff in 1958. But hot tips Tony Doherty and Kevin Evans were each halted by over-zealous doctors and a largely unknown 22-year-old from Cwmbran was the last man standing.

Thirteen years earlier, Jamie Arthur, like so many boxers, had turned to the sport to deal with school bullies. Under Chris Manley's tuition at Coed Eva ABC, he had enjoyed success as a junior and with the rebel ABF before a ceasefire between the warring groups allowed him to become Welsh ABA lightweight champion in 2002, just in time for the Manchester games.

But Arthur had lost twice at the Four Nations event in Killarney and then he drew Scot Mark Hastie, who had defeated him in the third-place box-off, as his first foe in the big one. But Jamie, knowing that he had barely tried in their previous

Jamie Arthur

meeting, went out confidently to storm through to the next round. Men from Lesotho, Malaysia and Botswana were seen off before the Welsh underdog took on Zambian southpaw Dennis Zimba in the final.

Arthur, allowed to box with a plaster covering a cut on his nose, took the action to the taller African, his flurries impressing the judges more

Jamie wins Commonwealth gold

than Zimba's single shots. The pair were level at halfway, but Jamie built a five-point lead in the third and defied Dennis's efforts in the last to emerge with a 37-35 victory. The Zambian camp were furious, but the gold was heading for Cwmbran.

The winner briefly considered trying for an Olympic place two years later, but common sense kicked in. Any switch to the pros had to happen while his name was in the headlines and Jamie opted to sign for Frank Warren.

He made his bow in the land of his birth – he was born in Aberdeen, when father Gordon was working on the oil rigs – outscoring journeyman Daniel Thorpe in Glasgow. He extended his winning streak to nine, including an appearance in Germany on a Johnny Nelson undercard. But fortune deserted him when he faced fellow Manchester gold medallist Haider Ali at Bridgend, a clash of heads leaving a gash over the Welshman's left eye severe enough for referee Wynford Jones to call a halt in the third.

By the time he reappeared, Arthur had linked up with Enzo Calzaghe, claiming his new mentor had taken him back to basics. Alas, his first outing with the charismatic Sardinian saw him floored three times and halted by Midlands-based South African Harry Ramogoadi. His pre-fight routine upset when his Edinburgh hotel room was not ready when he arrived, Jamie at least landed often enough himself to break Ramogoadi's jaw and condemn him to a night in a local hospital.

The second successive defeat triggered a release clause in his contract with Frank Warren and the promoter duly let him go. Arthur, deep in debt, promptly retired to seek a more reliable source of income, opening a gym in Cwmbran (later in Newport) and teaching in schools.

Three years later he was back, Chris Sanigar holding the management reins while a series of trainers including Tony Borg, Eddie Avoth, Steve

Sims and Darren Wilson handled the day-to-day work. After a routine rust-remover, the returnee challenged Welsh super-feather king Dai Davies at the Newport Centre on July 12, 2008. The occasionally fragile Merthyr man had been stopped twice in four successive losses – all in good class – and his lack of confidence was clear as Jamie dropped him with a body shot and the belt changed hands in the second.

Arthur had been barely over the featherweight limit and it was in the lower division that an eliminator decision over unbeaten Londoner Akaash Bhatia earned him a crack at British champion Martin Lindsay at Leigh on March 19, 2010. But he never recovered from two second-round knockdowns and the Ulsterman moved to 16-0 with a wide, unanimous verdict.

The Cwmbran redhead opted for a further drop in weight, entering a super-bantam Prizefighter tournament at the York Hall, only to lose a semi-final to another Welshman, unbeaten Ricky Owen. Yet it was Jamie who faced awkward Scot Kris Hughes for the vacant Commonwealth 8st 10lb throne at a London nightclub on October 16, 2010.

It was far from a classic, but Arthur's desire made the difference. His rival, from Bellshill, built an early lead, with Jamie needing ace cutman Mick Williamson to control a wound over the left eye from the second round onwards. But the middle sessions saw the tide turn and, despite losing two points for low blows, Arthur had the vote of all three judges to become the first Welsh boxer to reign both as amateur and pro over those places once coloured red on the map.

British champion Jason Booth had relinquished the Commonwealth crown to pursue world title dreams, but was promptly given a chance to regain it in a short-notice dual-title showdown at the Brentwood International Centre on February 5, 2011.

The Monmouthshire boxer used his five-inch height advantage to control the early stages, but Booth began to work his way inside and dominated the next few rounds, during which both were cut. Jamie battled back desperately, but the

Arthur floors unbeaten Scott Quigg on the way to a controversial defeat

33-year-old Nottingham warrior would not be denied and scraped a split-decision victory.

Arthur, once again, announced his retirement, but when fast-rising Scott Quigg, who had dethroned Booth, offered him another shot at the Lonsdale Belt, he quickly changed his mind. The pair met in a hotel built into the Bolton Wanderers football ground, one day short of a year since the challenger's last outing.

With 23 straight wins to his name, Quigg was a massive favourite, but Arthur almost upset the applecart in the fourth, dropping him with a solid left. The Bury boy recovered well and soon took command, but the end came in controversial fashion early in the eighth. Scott dug a painful left into Jamie's body, prompting him to drop his hands and spin around, momentarily turning his back. Referee Mark Green took this as a sign of surrender and leapt in to stop matters just as the Welshman was facing the right way again.

For all the protests, Arthur had once again come second in a British title fight. And once again he called it a day, focussing his attention on developing his new gym in Rhydyfelin. There was one further appearance late in 2015, when he took all six rounds against Croatian Antonio Horvatic in an exercise designed in part to show his new pupils that what he was teaching them worked.

The itch duly scratched, Jamie hung up the gloves again and concentrated on his day job as a draughtsman, while continuing to pass on his ring wisdom to the next generation.

JOHNNY BASHAM
(1889-1947)

🥊 **European Welterweight Champion 1919-1920**

🥊 **Empire Welterweight Champion 1919-1920**

🥊 **British Welterweight Champion 1914-1920**

🥊 **European Middleweight Champion 1921**

🥊 **British Middleweight Champion 1921**

It took a while for the citizens of Newport to pay their full respect to the greatest boxer their town ever produced. In Wrexham, where he was based while in the Army, they honoured him as one of their own. But, despite his return home when he left the forces, his achievements were barely acknowledged.

Though there was a huge turnout at his funeral, his burial place was first unmarked, then indicated by no more than a wooden cross. Four decades after his death, money was finally raised to provide a headstone worthy of a local legend.

After all, John Michael Basham was the first Welshman to claim British titles at two different weights. And he repeated that achievement at European level, becoming the first champion from his nation in each division.

The story began in the Crindau area, where he was raised in Ailesbury Street, one of the eight surviving children of a Kent-born labourer. Young Johnny sold newspapers on the streets to earn some spare cash before finding a job at a glassworks, where he used to spar with his colleagues on the night shift – until he was sacked after sneaking off without permission to take on a local rival. At 20 he was getting paid for his punches. But his was no easy road to the top.

Johnny Basham

Three stoppage defeats helped prompt him to enlist in the Royal Welsh Fusiliers, who promptly posted him to Wrexham, where his commanding officer encouraged his ring exploits. With only one points loss – to Sheffield's Gus Platts in Cardiff – in his first couple of years in uniform, Basham began to build a reputation.

There were setbacks, of course, but against top men. Recent Freddie Welsh victim Matt Wells knocked him out, while another East Ender, Charlie Wood, usually billed as 'Young Nipper', and a couple of Americans, Joe Hirst and Frank Madole, also claimed victory. Basham never met Hirst again, but was to claim revenge over Wood, Madole, Wells and our old friend Platts. The rematch with the red-haired Yorkshireman was, in effect, an eliminator for the British welter title and a packed Liverpool Stadium saw a thriller in which Johnny had to climb off the deck to earn his 20-round verdict.

Prior to that Basham had to go through his worst nightmare as a fighter. Barely a week after his marriage to Wrexham girl Winnie, he took on Harry Price, a New York-based South African. After 11 unremarkable rounds, the Welshman floored Price twice, the second occasion seeing his head bounce off the boards. Harry failed to regain consciousness and was ferried in a horse-drawn ambulance to Liverpool Royal Infirmary. Back at the Stadium, two policemen climbed through the ropes to confiscate Johnny's gloves and wraps, before accompanying him to Dale Street Police Station, where he was charged with causing grievous bodily harm.

When Price died during the night, the charge was upgraded to manslaughter, but an inquest two weeks later returned a verdict of misadventure and, as a result, the police offered no evidence against Johnny.

The Newport man returned to the ring and a series of successes saw him head for London's National Sporting Club on December 14, 1914, to contest the vacant welter throne with a former occupant, Middlesbrough-born Londoner Johnny Summers, who had also reigned at featherweight and seen a bid at lightweight repelled by Freddie Welsh. Summers was nearly 32, Basham just turned 25; the Welsh Johnny was also three inches taller.

Summers dropped the Gwent fighter early on for a count of nine, removing several teeth in the process, but the third brought a complete reversal of fortunes. The soldier – by now a sergeant – took total control, finally decking Summers twice in the ninth. On the second occasion, he was unable to beat the count.

Points wins over Summers and former conqueror Wells confirmed his status before Johnny returned to the NSC and his first official defence, against another ex-ruler, Plymouth-Irishman Tom McCormick, with whom he had earlier drawn. After a one-sided contest, Basham ended matters in the 13th. Next up, in Liverpool, was Caerau's skilful Dai Roberts, whose renowned defensive wizardry could not prevent a seventh-round knockout in a bout billed as for the title, although not recognised as such by the all-powerful NSC. Both McCormick and Roberts were to die in the trenches.

Basham (right) defeats Matt Wells in the triple-title clash

Although his native Switzerland was neutral, Albert Badoud spent the war years in Britain, his frequent outings at Liverpool Stadium including two points losses to Basham. But when the pair returned there on October 21, 1915, to contest the European title and a £500 purse, things turned out differently. Badoud controlled matters from the first bell, flooring Basham twice before dispatching him in the ninth. There was talk of Johnny having been ill in the lead-up to the fight, but it was still a major shock.

Basham and other boxers, including Jim Driscoll and Jimmy Wilde, were drafted into a special elite corps and taken on morale-boosting trips behind the lines. While he never actually battled the Germans, among those who sparred with him were the poet and novelist Robert Graves and the future King Edward VIII, then Prince of Wales.

In more serious combat, Johnny was unbeaten for nearly five years, during which he added two more belts to his collection, including the European honour. This time French war hero Francis Charles was the opponent at London's Olympia on September 2, 1919. At first Johnny found the visitor's crouching style difficult to handle, but he was generally in command and, despite a seventh-round knockdown, emerged with a clear decision at the end of 20 rounds.

The Empire honour followed two months later, in a rubber match with old foe Wells. With the Lonsdale Belt also at stake at Holborn Stadium, Matt swapped his usual long-distance boxing for hooks in an attempt to negate Johnny's reach advantage, but to no avail.

Basham put his three titles on the line in the first of four shuddering collisions with the phenomenal Ted 'Kid' Lewis, an East Ender who had spent the war years in North America, twice winning and losing the world welter crown in a classic series of scraps with New Yorker Jack Britton.

On his return to London, he won the British middleweight crown before dropping down to face Basham at Olympia on June 9, 1920. In a sense the fight was over inside three rounds: the first saw a left hook open a cut on Johnny's right cheek, while the third brought a worse injury to the Welshman's mouth, possibly caused by an errant elbow. Blood poured

Johnny under fire in the second fight with Ted 'Kid' Lewis

continuously from the damage until cornerman Danny Davies pulled him out at the end of the ninth, much to his man's disgust.

A rematch was arranged for the Albert Hall, five months later, with British and European honours at stake. Basham, who struggled to make weight, still held his own for the first dozen sessions. By the 13th, however, he was bleeding from the left ear and the 'Kid' was scoring more freely. An uppercut floored Johnny early in the 19th; when another flurry of blows felled Johnny again, he rose, only to stagger across the ring, hands down, prompting referee Eugene Corri to step in amid confusion. Corri claimed the timekeeper had reached 10. That worthy denied it. But Johnny, with impressive sportsmanship, accepted the ending with a shrug, adding, "It's Ted's night out, that's all."

Basham announced his retirement, but soon reconsidered and opted for a move up to middle, where the British and European crowns were worn by old pal Platts. When the pair faced each other for a fourth time before a sellout crowd at the Albert Hall on May 31, 1921, Gus won the first, but that was pretty much it for the Yorkshireman. He made matters competitive throughout, but Basham took the decision by a street to make history as Wales's first two-weight ruler. It was, however, his last taste of victory.

That man Lewis was also back at middle and challenged Johnny for his new honours five months later, again at the Albert Hall. This time Basham looked a shadow of his old self, allowing the Londoner to force the pace throughout. Courage and conditioning kept the Welshman going until the 11th, when he was dropped, and another knockdown in the next was followed by a sustained barrage which saw the towel float in from the champion's corner.

Johnny took a year out, but the arrival in Britain of Irish-born American Mike McTigue, later to reign over the world's light-heavyweights, tempted him back to the ring. Reports of partying in London three weeks before their date in Sheffield hardly inspired confidence among Basham's backers:

McTigue duly finished him in three.

Two years later Basham, back in Newport after leaving the Army, was persuaded to face fellow-townsman and former Wales rugby star Jerry Shea at Stow Hill Pavilion in a show to raise money for the Royal Gwent Hospital. Shea, though never in Johnny's league as a boxer, was the fitter man and took a 15-round decision. The winner never fought again; the loser, desperate for money, had one more attempt at Lewis, almost a decade after their first clash.

Three months beyond his 40th birthday, Basham went to his inevitable fate at the Hoxton Baths in Lewis's heartland. The 'Kid', himself 36 and in his last bout, dropped his faded foe in the second and opened a cut over his left eye. To the relief of ringsiders, the injury gave the referee to chance to call a halt in the third.

The local hero now has a proper gravestone

Exhibitions in village halls throughout the Valleys paid some bills, as did a stint as a London fireman and as a barman at a friend's pub in the Durham coalfield. The jobs, like the cash, did not last long. Yet he retained the twinkle in his eye that had earned him the tag of 'The Happy Warrior'.

But his health deteriorated and he died of a seizure at his Mountjoy Place home, just eight days before a tournament intended to provide him with a pension fund.

NICK BIRCH
(1894-1960)

🥊 Welsh Heavyweight Champion 1917-20

It was always likely the fair-haired, blue-eyed youngster would be a performer of some sort. After all, his Cockney father, William, used to give his occupation as "comedian". And Nick's big sister, Rose, became a tightrope walker in a circus.

There was tragedy as well as comedy in the Birch household, however. William and his Berkshire-born wife Sarah had 11 children in all; only four survived their early years. The family moved around Britain – Nick was born at Llanelly, not the coastal town, but the village near Brynmawr – before settling at Cwmfelinfach, where his father became a caretaker at the colliery offices and his son, on leaving school, began work as an "oiler of trams" on the pit surface.

He developed into a fine figure of a man, who soon showed he could handle himself in a rumble. Back in the early years of the competition the Welsh amateur championships had only a handful of classes, with nothing higher than middleweight. A Machen businessman who had seen Birch in the gym introduced him to influential Cardiff journalist Charlie Barnett, who urged the Welsh ABA to introduce a heavyweight division. They agreed – and then rejected Birch's entry because his form had been filled in wrongly! Nick duly turned pro.

The only setbacks early on came when a couple of referees took exception to the rougher elements of Birch's activity, the second disqualification coming for holding against Pontypool rugby forward George Oliver. But that was that, ringwise, for a full year.

After serving nearly four years in the Territorial Army, he was released on medical grounds – he was suffering from synovitis in his right knee, originally damaged when he fell into a sump at the pit – but was back in khaki in early 1916. This time he lasted less than a year, being discharged as "no longer physically fit for war". Within five months he was Welsh heavyweight champion!

Domestically, Welsh titles were very loosely organised: in effect, anyone could claim one, but general acceptance required a significant success or two against fellow-countrymen. Birch

Nick Birch

achieved that recognition following a return against Oliver at the Cwmfelinfach Workmen's Hall on March 31, 1917, emerging with a 15-round decision and, with it, acknowledgement that he was the best in Wales.

Oliver went on to win four international caps as a second row in 1920, prompting a move to Hull and a rugby league career which also saw him represent his country. His boxing was a thing of the past; Birch, on the other hand, began to showcase his wares in London, picking up extra publicity – he was referred to as a "white hope", although in Britain it hardly had the racial significance that gave birth to the phrase in the US – by boxing exhibitions with Llew Edwards, on the brink of the British featherweight title, and, more physically challenging, heavyweight king Bombardier Billy Wells.

In competitive action, Nick stopped former South African heavy ruler Harry Smith and outpointed Portsmouth's Gordon Sims despite an injured left arm – his "sinister weapon", as *Boxing* described it – but Mancunian Jack Curphey knocked him out in front of the dinner-jacketed members of the National Sporting Club.

Back home Birch saw off Joe Knight, from his own village, and Ivor James, the contests regarded as title defences simply because it was impossible for a heavyweight to have an over-the-limit bout and, in theory, he could lose his crown any time he met a fellow-Welshman.

A more serious challenger was Abertillery's George Partridge, but when Nick travelled up the valley to meet him he floored George three times and forced him to retire after eight rounds.

By now Birch was having increasing problems with his hands, twice being forced to quit against former British light-heavy claimant Bandsman Dick Rice, and when he was beaten in three rounds by future British and Empire heavyweight boss Phil Scott – then still campaigning under his real surname, Suffling – it seems to have been the last straw.

In later life he moved to England, dying at Hampstead at the age of 65.

RONNIE BISHOP
(1916-1986)

🥊 Welsh Flyweight Champion 1939-40

A n English crowd may not have cared who won the Welsh flyweight title fight before them. But when it finished they were left in no doubt how much it mattered to the victor.

When Bob Hill indicated that Ronnie Bishop had done enough to dethrone Swansea's Jackie Kiley, the Markham boy went wild. He danced around the ring in jubilation, kissing everyone he met on the way: his trainer, his seconds, his opponent, HIS trainer and seconds, even one highly embarrassed referee!

And 4,000 fans at Gloucester's Kingsholm rugby ground cheered him to the echo.

It all seemed rather unlikely when he was halted in five rounds by Pengam's Ken Evans in his pro debut three years earlier. But Bishop was to lose only once more – on points to ringwise Danny Andrews, from Treharris – in his next 18 contests, although there were a fair number of draws along the way. Most of his action was in the Valleys; his title bid marked only the third time he had ventured across the border.

Ronnie was a big underdog when he entered the ring on July 10, 1939. The classy Kiley had drawn and won in previous meetings between them, and the first session went the champion's way. But the Gwent man shrugged off his nerves and set a demanding pace, which Jackie found it difficult to match. A cut below the challenger's left eye, the result of a fifth-round head clash, slowed him somewhat, Kiley taking the initiative and targeting the injury.

But once he realised the damage was not severe enough to stop the bout, Bishop redoubled his efforts and, ignoring the Swansea fighter's height and reach advantage, waded in to attack the body. It was clearly an area in which Kiley was vulnerable and, with his tormentor rarely letting up, there was little he could do to stave off the inevitable defeat and his conqueror's delirious celebration.

Ronnie Bishop

Bishop did well to enjoy his moment in the sun. He was not to win a single fight as champion, with no fewer than four Welshmen among his conquerors before the affronted Kiley was given a shot at his old belt on May 13, 1940, promoter Jack Matthews staging boxing for the first time at Crumlin's Palace cinema.

Because of the war the traditional Whit Monday holiday had been cancelled, so the main event started at 7.15pm to accommodate those scheduled to work the night shift. Given his recent form, few were surprised when Ronnie was clearly outpointed, his "hurricane tactics" never enough to unsettle the Swansea man.

Bishop's bobbing style frequently baffled opponents unfamiliar with him, but in later years it did not take them long to work him out. Victories became rare and although he invariably put up a decent show he had become little more than a journeyman.

For a while his only successes came in trips to the West of England; domestic rivals tended to come out on top. No doubt feeling that if he was going to lose he might as well earn a few quid, Bishop began to travel, Scotland and Northern Ireland joining various parts of England on his itinerary, while future world champion Terry Allen, world challenger Joe Curran and British feather king Ronnie Clayton were among his conquerors.

There were a couple of stoppage wins in Watford over pre-war Welsh fly ruler Pat Warburton, but they reflected the decline of the 35-year-old Ebbw Vale man more than a sudden resurgence in Bishop's fortunes. Warburton never boxed again and in early 1948 Ronnie joined him in retirement after being halted in four by a former jockey from Trethomas, Jackie Hodder. Ironically, it took place in Gloucester, the city that had witnessed his greatest triumph.

ABNER BLACKSTOCK
(1959-)

🥊 Welsh Cruiserweight Champion 1986-1990

With only two participants, boxing is not really a sport in which one man can find himself surrounded. Yet it must have felt like that for Rhondda boy Les Davies when he faced Abner Blackstock.

Their showdown at Risca Leisure Centre on May 23, 1986, was the first for a Welsh title in the recently introduced cruiserweight division. The pair had met twice before: Davies had beaten him in the Welsh ABAs, but the Jamaican-born Newport machinist earned his revenge in his paid debut at Blaenavon Leisure Centre.

Abner – his real name was Lloyd, but nobody ever called him that – had twice won Welsh amateur titles before taking the plunge with Cardiff manager Mac Williams at the age of 26. After the successful bow against Davies, he had won two and lost two before the old rivals met again. It was the night Blackstock reached a level he had never reached before – and would never replicate.

Abner Blackstock

With height and reach on his side, Abner was also more mobile than the somewhat static carpenter from Cymmer, with a flexibility in his upper body that enabled him to sway around his foe in bewildering fashion. Each time Les tried to move inside those long arms, the Pill man countered him with solid rights. And when Davies stood off, Blackstock pulled new tricks from his extensive armoury.

The third saw him switch to southpaw, land two rights on Les's face and then go back to the orthodox stance. In the seventh, he brought his right down to his hip, nodded towards it, shrugged his shoulders and whipped it up beneath the guard to jolt Davies's blond head back. It was a breathtaking performance.

The game Rhondda fighter plodded on, resigned to defeat but determined to last the course. Even that small consolation was to be denied him: he launched a desperate assault in the ninth and ran on to Abner's right cross, which sent him stumbling into the ropes. Les took a short count before his tormentor stormed back in and referee Ivor Bassett stepped between them.

For the loser, the defeat had been so one-sided that he never boxed again. Yet the winner,

Blackstock (right) ties up Tee Jay

whose display had promised a bright future, had reached his summit. He lost a drab British title eliminator to former conqueror Roy Smith, travelled to Copenhagen to be stopped by Norway's future WBO cruiser king Magne Havnå, and then dropped a decision to Londoner Derek Angol, later to challenge for that same WBO crown.

The pattern was set: Abner followed the money and came out the wrong side of a series of clashes with some decent operators, among them former European boss Richard Caramanolis, undefeated Italian Olympian Luigi Gaudiano and British champions Tee Jay and Andrew Straughn.

A rare exception to this miserable litany came thanks to wily manager Williams. Before Blackstock met Panamanian southpaw Víctor Córdoba in his adopted Belfast, they found themselves in adjacent dressing rooms and Mac took full advantage. He picked up a chair and started hitting the dividing wall, shouting, "Stop it, Abner, wait for the fight!" As Córdoba, a future WBA titleholder, left for the ring, Williams held Blackstock back, telling him, "You'll get to him soon enough!" The Central American, totally spooked and thinking he was in with a madman, went berserk in his attempts to end it early and wound up being disqualified in the second for thumping Abner in the groin.

There were a few lucrative, if painful trips to Belgium and the Netherlands as the Newport fighter accepted the role of international journeyman, before a detached retina, suffered while sparring, brought down the curtain. Despite a surgeon's assertion that he could resume boxing, the Board, after listening to alternative opinions, refused him a licence.

In enforced retirement Abner helped coach local youngsters for two decades until further eye trouble put an end to that as well. But he can always remember one night in Risca when he touched the heights.

ASHLEY BRACE
(1991-)

🥊 **WBC International Bantamweight Champion 2017-**

🥊 **European Youth Bronze Medallist 2008**

The old-timer sitting at ringside in the gleaming new Ebbw Vale Leisure Centre could not get his head around it. A woman was topping the bill! He sat quietly enjoying the undercard and then Ashley Brace arrived to the acclaim of her townsfolk. Within a couple of rounds he was urging her on with the best of them.

That night, April 22, 2017, saw female boxing take a huge step forward as Brace halted former world title challenger Alexandra Vlajk to claim the vacant WBC International belt. That it took until the ninth of the scheduled 10 rounds was down to the incredible courage and durability of the 37-year-old Hungarian – and, less admirably, the stubbornness of a second who should have pulled her out much earlier.

After a fairly tentative opening, Ashley, who had to shed a surplus pound at the weigh-in, used her speed and movement to dominate throughout. The way her victory was received underlined the readiness of the Welsh public to accept her as a talented boxer and not as some sort of novelty act.

Ashley Brace

It also marked a complete turnaround in the career of the teaching assistant from Rassau, who had plumbed the depths before the 2014 Commonwealth Games. Having edged out hot favourite Lynsey Holdaway to win a Welsh title and claim a place at the Glasgow event, where female boxing was included for the first time, she was shockingly ruled ineligible by the international body, AIBA, for participating in a world kick-boxing championship the previous year.

The Welsh ABA, who had taken Brace to the pre-Games training camp in Canada, admitted that it had failed to pass on her application for reinstatement, with the result that she missed out on her chance to make history.

A kick-boxer at eight, Ashley turned to the orthodox version at 15, quickly earning selection for the Wales team at the European Youth championships in 2008, returning with a bronze medal. She graduated to a Welsh senior title at lightweight, in the vest of the Heads of the Valleys club, but defeat in the following year's final by Becky Price and rejection by the Team GB set-up meant she switched back to kick-boxing for two years.

Ashley celebrates with her team (from left): father Shaun, Chris Sanigar, Tony Borg and Billy Reynolds

She returned in 2014 with Torfaen ABC, slimming down to flyweight – one of only three weight divisions for women in Glasgow – to upset the experienced Holdaway and then be let down by official incompetence. The disillusionment played its part in Ashley's decision to turn pro with Bristol-based Chris Sanigar, while Tony Borg took charge of her training, alongside her father, Shaun.

After two points wins – her debut in Newport was the first Board-licensed female bout in Wales – Ashley began to develop her power, knocking out Romanian Gabriella Mezei and becoming the first in seven years and 65 fights to stop Slovakian Claudia Ferenczi.

It was time to face tougher challenges. First up, at the Rhondda Fach Sports Centre, was Galina Koleva, a Bulgarian who had worn WBC and IBF world belts, as well as an interim WBA strap. Brace beat her without losing a round. It was a victory that prompted Sanigar to showcase her against Vlajk in the first pro show in Ebbw Vale for 17 years.

The event also introduced her to a wider public, with highlights shown on S4C, and a month later there was UK-wide TV exposure when Ashley appeared at Cardiff's Motorpoint Arena on a bill organised by Cyclone Promotions, the company founded by former world champion Barry McGuigan. She took her new status in her stride, winning all six rounds against former world title challenger Nevenka Mikulic, from Croatia.

The girl who calls herself 'Storm' is set to blow the minds of more traditionalists over the next few years. And one old-timer in particular will be cheering her all the way.

DON BRAITHWAITE
(1937-2017)

🥊 Empire Games Bronze Medallist 1958

Training regularly with the outstanding talent of his generation was always going to benefit the Caerphilly boy's career. But his encounters with Howard Winstone went beyond sparring sessions: the pair even ended up sleeping together!

All above board, of course. But when the Welsh amateur team headed for Belgium for an international match the hotel's rooms only had double beds, so all the boys had to pile in.

At least when it came to the Empire Games, there was enough space at RAF St Athan, which served as the athletes' village, for everyone to have his own bunk, but once again Don Braithwaite roomed with his mate Howie. And both picked up medals for the host country.

Don began boxing at the age of 11, joining Caerphilly ABC, where he was trained by Ted Timms and Doug Lawrence. And it was not long before he and Winstone, already among the best youngsters around, were visiting each other's gyms to swap punches on a weekly basis.

In 1958, Braithwaite entered the Welsh ABAs for the first time. With the Games heading for Cardiff later in the summer, the title race was particularly hard-fought, with a record postwar entry for the single-day tournament at the old Drill Hall in Dumfries Place.

A first-round knockout took Don into the final, where he outpointed Winstone's Dowlais clubmate, Don James, and although he was outpointed in the British, the crew-cut 21-year-old was still named for the year's big event. Unusually for the period, the squad had a fortnight's camp prior to the Games, although the authorities still vetoed plans to spar with pros at Benny Jacobs's gym.

The small field at flyweight meant Don only needed one victory to guarantee a place on the podium. And he duly achieved it, coming through impressively on points after a thriller against Rhodesian Bill Pretorius. That brought him up against a skilful Scot, 23-year-old Jackie Brown, who had beaten Liverpool's highly touted Tommy Bache in the British final a couple of months before.

There was a setback when the Welshman was found to be half a pound over the limit at the morning weigh-in. He shed the surplus in time, but never found his rhythm and suffered a cut on the right cheek. He did hurt Brown with a left hook in the last, only for the Leith man to avoid any recurrence and reach the bell with a clear lead. Jackie went on to repeat his win over Bache and claim gold before a pro career which saw him become British and Commonwealth flyweight champion.

Don Braithwaite

Braithwaite – like room-mate Winstone, who won Wales's only gold in any sport – was a man in demand. Johnny Lewis, the Welsh-speaking Cockney who trained Dick Richardson, travelled to Caerphilly to see Don and persuaded him to join the Newport heavyweight in the Wally Lesley camp.

Unfortunately, he was not to match the success of his pal Howie, despite packing 27 bouts into three years. He won 13 of them, the highlight coming when he travelled to London to end the unbeaten record of West Ham hopeful Brian Bissmire. But the East Ender gained his revenge and began an eight-fight winless streak for Don. The decision to retire was, however, taken out of his hands.

A blacksmith's striker at Windsor Colliery, Abertridwr, in his amateur days, Braithwaite was refused time off for an international fixture. Bob Lewis, later to own the Club Double Diamond, offered him a job with his concrete firm and always supported his boxing.

In 1963 the brakes failed on a dumper truck he was driving at work, and Don suffered severe brain damage in the resultant crash. He spent nearly a year in hospital and, although he made a complete recovery, he was firmly warned off any return to the ring.

Instead he turned to training, setting up Wingfield ABC in the Llanbradach pub run by father Reg, and looking after the likes of Tony Davies and Kelvin Smart. His service to the sport was recognised with a BEM in 2015.

JOE CALZAGHE
(1972-)

- 🥊 **'Ring' Light-Heavyweight Champion 2008**

- 🥊 **'Ring' Super-Middleweight Champion 2006-08**

- 🥊 **WBO Super-Middleweight Champion 1997-2008**

- 🥊 **WBC Super-Middleweight Champion 2007-08**

- 🥊 **WBA Super-Middleweight Champion 2007-08**

- 🥊 **IBF Super-Middleweight Champion 2006-07**

- 🥊 **British Super-Middleweight Champion 1995-97**

He ruled the planet at two weights, held a world title for an incredible 11 years and never lost a professional fight. That is a record no other British boxer can match. Yet for much of his career there were many unwilling to give the Newbridge southpaw even grudging respect.

Everything changed in Manchester in the small hours of March 5, 2006. In the US, where the disparaging view of Joe Calzaghe was almost unanimous, Jeff Lacy was regarded as the second coming of Ali, Tyson, Holyfield – name your fistic idol, Lacy was his natural heir. And even in Britain, those who had watched on television as Jeff floored Robin Reid four times on the way to a first-ever stoppage loss bought into the hype. Bookies here had the Florida fighter 4-1 on to defeat the man who had never been defeated. Even the trade paper, *Boxing News*, tipped the American.

In retrospect, it seems incredible. For Calzaghe was pitch-perfect: from the first bell to the last, Lacy was helpless to evade the punches coming his way, incapable of landing the 'Left Hook' of his nickname. Two cards of 119-107 and another of 119-105 underlined the Welshman's supremacy, even though there was only one knockdown, in the last. The solitary point dropped came after Californian referee Raul Caiz penalised Joe for playfully flicking a left hand behind his back when the IBF champion's head was lodged under his right armpit.

In a crowded press conference, those Lacy camp members who had dismissed Calzaghe as a "slapper" were fulsome in their praise for the man they had maligned.

"I haven't ever seen a better performance. Joe was a master of distance, of timing, of angles," proclaimed a stunned Dan Birmingham, recently honoured as US Trainer of the Year. His opposite number, Enzo Calzaghe, was to be rewarded as the best coach – across all sports – at the next BBC Sports Personality of the Year ceremony, with Joe winning the public vote for the main award.

Joe Calzaghe and father Enzo

They had both come a long way since Enzo took his nine-year-old son to a corrugated shack alongside Newbridge rugby ground to be introduced to life in the ring. The unsung Paul Williams was his early guide, while trips to Newport allowed extra instruction from former British champion Steve Sims. Meanwhile the senior Calzaghe, a Sardinian-born musician who had never boxed competitively, was picking things up as quickly as his boy. Before long, Dad had taken over the show and Joe was collecting trophies.

There was a scare at 15, when he damaged ligaments in his right wrist and a doctor at the Royal Gwent told him his boxing days were over. It was 18 months before he returned, reaching the Welsh senior final, where he lost a thriller to Barry's Michael Smyth, before a trip to the European Junior Championships in Prague saw him edged out by Romanian Adrian Opreda, who went on to take the gold.

It was the last time Joe Calzaghe knew failure.

The 1992 Olympics were in his sights, but he was a growing lad. After winning the British ABAs at welter in 1991, he moved up to light-middle and beat future WBC super-middle king Glenn Catley in the final. But the Welsh ABA, miffed by Joe's frequent pull-outs from the national team, decided to send Rhoose's Matthew Turner to the Olympic qualifiers; Turner was beaten by the aforementioned Reid

Calzaghe (left) beats Darren Dorrington to win his third British ABA title

and the Englishman went on to secure a seat on the plane and a bronze medal in Barcelona. The Calzaghes were certain Joe would have struck gold!

There was a final season as an amateur, with the Welshman, now at middle, becoming only the second boxer to claim three successive ABA titles at different weights. It was time to go pro. Mickey Duff was chosen to guide the youngster he called "the best amateur to come out of the UK in 10 years". And it was straight into the big time.

World heavyweight champion Lennox Lewis was defending against Frank Bruno at a damp National Stadium in Cardiff; Joe made his bow on the undercard, halting Brummie Paul Hanlon in the opener. In fact, of his first nine contests only former Foreign Legionnaire Spencer Alton and pineapple-haired Trevor Ambrose made it into the second round. The much heavier Bobbi Joe Edwards became the first to take Calzaghe the distance – the second to do so, 13 bouts later, was Edwards's cousin, Chris Eubank.

In between, the Newbridge southpaw became the first Welshman to hold the British super-middleweight title, picking apart another former amateur ace, Scot Stephen Wilson, at the Albert Hall on October 28, 1995, for an eighth-round stoppage and the belt vacated by Ulsterman Sam Storey. The sport's writers chose Joe as Young Boxer of the Year and he then defied Mark Delaney's hostile fans at Brentwood, dismissing the Essex fighter's challenge in five rounds. But six days before a defence against Liverpool's Paul Wright he turned an ankle while running and had to pull out.

Fed up with facing poor Americans on untelevised cards, Calzaghe had become disillusioned with Duff and co-manager Terry Lawless, especially as Mickey admitted that Yorkshire gipsy Henry Wharton was ahead of him in the queue for international honours. He jumped ship – costing him a substantial sum and his domestic crown – and signed with Frank Warren, who brought Sky coverage and promised a world title shot if he won three more fights.

Joe duly did so, his victims including unbeaten Welsh-American Tyler

Joe's straight right sees off Stephen Wilson

Hughes, later seen in front of the hotel television, taking photos of himself on the canvas to show folks back in Nebraska that he had been knocked out by a future world champion! Warren kept his word and Calzaghe was named to challenge WBO boss Steve Collins at Sheffield Arena on October 11, 1997. But the Dubliner, claiming a foot injury, stunned an awards dinner by announcing his immediate retirement from the ring; his predecessor, Eubank, who had been campaigning at light-heavy, vowed that he could make 12st in the two weeks remaining and was drafted in to contest the newly empty throne.

The Brighton braggart had been an outstanding champion and, despite the short notice, was expected by several good judges – including *Boxing News* editor Claude Abrams, who forecast a stoppage win – to know too much for a largely untested opponent. By the end of the first round, many had changed their minds. Within 15 seconds of the post-midnight start, Eubank found himself on the canvas, stunned by an overhand left and listening to American Joe Cortez count to eight. He rose, eyes clear, and grinned, but Calzaghe, any pre-fight

Calzaghe beats Eubank to claim the WBO belt

nerves dispelled, dominated the round, even throwing in an Ali shuffle.

Eubank, his physical strength matched by an unbending will, stayed in contention, but Joe's speed and mobility left the older man unable to make serious inroads into the contest. He paid another brief visit to the deck in the 10th, but it was Calzaghe, in unfamiliar territory, who suddenly appeared vulnerable in the closing seconds. Two solid rights had him hanging on at the final bell, but victory was secure, the three British judges favouring him by margins of five, seven and nine points.

The 'Italian Stallion' – one of several nicknames coined over the years, none of which stuck – was WBO super-middleweight champion. He was to remain so through 21 defences and across a complete decade. Yet for much of that period he was being scorned for the standard of his opposition. There is truth in the allegation, but it was not always a case of risk-averse matchmaking. Calzaghe had five mandatory defences against the men the WBO installed at No 1 in their rankings: Juan Carlos Giménez, Rick Thornberry, Mario Veit (twice) and Mger Mkrtchian were all below world class, but needed to be dealt with if Joe wanted to keep his belt.

Then there were the late substitutes brought in to save a show or a TV date. Mediocre Americans Will McIntyre and Tocker Pudwill were only called up because the likes of two-time IBF challenger Antwun Echols, former WBC middle king Hassine Cherifi and multiple world title contender Thomas Tate opted out, claiming a variety of physical failings. Three-time WBA middle boss William Joppy was another reluctant to share a ring with the Newbridge fighter.

Calzaghe's own injury problems, particularly with his right wrist, were a regular feature. He pulled out of some fights, to the extent that staff at Sports Network dubbed him 'Sicknote', while on other occasions he entered the ring with little gym work behind him.

There had been a long layoff following further surgery before Joe faced Runcorn's Reid, who had followed his Olympic medal by winning the WBC crown, in Newcastle. The build-up was fraught: with no sparring, the Welshman misjudged his weight and had to shed six pounds in two hours before stepping on the scales. That evening he began eating an ice-cream at his hotel and found it was full of bits of glass, sparking a myriad conspiracy theories.

The bout itself had some equally unpalatable ingredients: Robin held repeatedly, used his shoulder and generally tried to rough Joe up, with referee Roy Francis belatedly docking him a point for a low blow in the eighth. But Calzaghe, who fractured a metacarpal in his left hand in the sixth, was open to a right throughout and boxed well below par. The three judges all returned cards of 116-111, two for the champion and the other for Reid, a disparity which reflected the difficulty in scoring many of the rounds in a close and hard-fought battle.

Joe's difficulties once again raised question marks over his insistence on staying at home with his father, whose own lack of ring experience had always drawn scorn from "old school" trainers across the border. This time Warren joined the chorus and lined up veteran Londoner George Francis to take

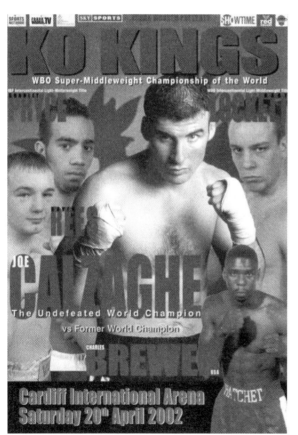

The Calzaghe v Brewer programme

control, while Enzo discovered the situation via the *Sun*. After a family heart-to-heart, plans to look elsewhere were shelved and the Calzaghe combo resumed the old routine.

But a new injury, to an elbow, hindered him during 12 tedious rounds in Manchester against negative East Anglian David Starie, with US channel Showtime in attendance as well as 20,000 fans waiting to see Mike Tyson flatten Julius Francis. Once again Calzaghe wanted time off to let it heal. Warren, increasingly frustrated at Joe's displays, told him he had to face Palestinian-American Omar Sheika in August come what may. And it proved to be a much better night, with Sheika rescued in the fifth, after which Joe revealed that he had solved the elbow problem – by giving up his regular trips to a nearby pitch-and-putt course!

Next up was another English ex-WBC ruler but there was one big difference, Where Reid and Calzaghe disliked one another, Richie Woodhall was a close friend from amateur days. But business is business and Joe dealt with it in 10 rounds.

The next serious challenger was to be Charles Brewer, a 32-year-old Philadelphian who had held the IBF's version of the title before losing two controversial split decisions in Germany to local hero Sven Ottke, a man who went through his own unbeaten career stubbornly unwilling to consider a unification bout with Joe. The Brewer fight was originally planned as the Welshman's US bow, but, with Showtime's production teams tied up by the Winter Olympics at Salt Lake City, it was back to the CIA. American viewers will still able to watch as Calzaghe strode to a wide unanimous decision after 12 exciting rounds.

Matters were briefer, but just as thrilling when another former world ruler crossed the Atlantic 14 months later. Byron Mitchell had twice worn the WBA belt and, like Brewer, had lost it on a split to the home-loving Ottke. Clearly unwilling to leave things to the judges, the 'Slamma from 'Bama' uncorked a right uppercut early in the second to drop Calzaghe to the canvas for the first time in his life. Joe leapt back into the fray and a left sent the American halfway through the

Calzaghe takes Jeff Lacy to school

ropes; when he fell backwards in his own corner under a merciless barrage from the champion, referee Dave Parris called a halt.

Calzaghe was to go down again in a mauling argument with Egyptian-born New Yorker Kabary Salem in Edinburgh, but won clearly and the powers-that-be were setting up a "career-defining" collision with Lacy. The choice of Denmark-based Kenyan Evans Ashira as a final warm-up opponent just eight weeks before proved disastrous. Ashira was well beaten, but his hard head left Joe with a broken left hand; when the Lacy fight was, inevitably, called off, it unleashed a predictable torrent of abuse for the Welshman, with "fraud" and "coward" among the more printable online comments.

Happily, Showtime were determined the showdown should happen, although even then it was a close thing. Three weeks before the rearranged Manchester date Joe left a Harley Street consulting room convinced that his troublesome wrist was too bad for him to contemplate fighting someone of Lacy's ability. It was only a vocal battering from his father, insisting that the Florida man was "made for him", that persuaded Calzaghe to go through with what proved his masterclass.

The IBF, whose belt Joe had acquired from Lacy, ordered him to defend against German Robert Stieglitz, but US television suits were not interested, so, after outpointing Aussie-African Sakio Bika, later to win the WBC crown, that particular strap was handed back. But two more were heading to Wales when Dane Mikkel Kessler brought the WBC and WBA versions to the Millennium Stadium for one of the greatest nights in Welsh sporting history.

A European indoor record 50,014 people packed the iconic venue in the middle of the night. They saw a titanic tussle, in which the unbeaten Kessler, seven years his junior, presented problems Joe had never before

encountered. After an even start, the half-English visitor – his mother is from Salisbury – stepped up the pace in the fourth and fifth, with Calzaghe's head frequently jolted backwards by right uppercuts as he moved in. But Joe changed his approach, standing off and boxing to take control around the halfway mark, Mikkel admitting later that he should have thrown more combinations when he was on top instead of going for power with single shots.

Millennium Mayhem - Joe drives Mikkel Kessler back

The finishing straight could have become something of a celebratory jaunt for the Welshman, but a weary Kessler was able to dig deep and provide a grandstand finish, with Calzaghe willingly drawn into toe-to-toe exchanges rather than protecting his clear lead. At the bell, the pair hugged, Joe kissing his rival's cheek before joining his jubilant team as Mikkel turned, head down, to

Hopkins floors Calzaghe in the opening round

his own despondent corner. The judges duly confirmed Calzaghe's superiority by four (twice) and five points, making him the first non-American at any weight to have held all four major world championship belts.

Warren, who described the night as "the best moment in all my years in boxing", promptly called out Bernard Hopkins, the legendary Philadelphian, who had once agreed to face Joe for $3m only to return the following day demanding double. This time, however, 'B-Hop' shared the enthusiasm, helping the publicity bandwagon on its way by telling Calzaghe, in Las Vegas for a Ricky Hatton fight, that he "would never lose to a white boy". And so the deal was done, with Calzaghe moving up, with a sigh of relief, to light-heavyweight. In this division, neither had a recognised title, but *Ring* magazine, whose super-middle belt been awarded to Joe when he beat Lacy, promptly put their light-heavy equivalent on the line.

The pair would meet at the Thomas and Mack Centre, Las Vegas, on April 19, 2008, the show being "hosted" by the Planet Hollywood casino and attracting a constellation of stars to ringside. Sylvester Stallone, Arnold Schwarzenegger and Bruce Willis sat alongside Ioan Gruffudd and Catherine Zeta-Jones, bedecked in the Welsh flag, while Sir Tom Jones sang *Hen Wlad fy Nhadau* and hundreds of travelling fans raised the roof with chants of "Super, super Joe, super Joe Calzaghe!"

But they were silenced in the first minute when a chopping right from the 43-year-old American dropped their idol. Up at three, Joe was unhurt, but the triumph handed a two-point start to the living legend in the other corner. 'B-Hop' had learned enough in a two-decade career not to become over-excited by his success, resuming a game plan directed more at restricting Calzaghe than initiating much positive activity himself.

Joe outboxes the legendary Roy Jones, Jr.

The next five sessions were closely contested, but as Hopkins began to tire so Joe's speed and accuracy became more evident. But when Michael Buffer, a week after surgery for throat cancer, announced the outcome Welsh supporters were shocked to hear that judge Adalaide Byrd gave it to the veteran by a point. Her two colleagues, however, also Americans, had the visitor in front by three and five points. The punch stats revealed that Calzaghe had landed 232 blows – more than any other boxer against Hopkins – to Bernard's meagre 127; the loser still claimed he was robbed!

For Calzaghe there remained just one ambition, an oft-mooted, never finalised meeting with the man he had once revered, Roy Jones, Jr. Previous negotiations had always broken down, but this time neither boxer was prepared to let that happen. Jones's eagerness for the bout was evident from his comments when he appeared as co-commentator on BBC Radio Wales's coverage of the Hopkins bout, while Joe had been calling him out for years.

Once again, talks between the rival promotional teams were getting nowhere. This time the pair decided to take matters into their own hands. Calzaghe's relationship with Warren was on its last legs and would end in court; Jones, similarly, was fed up with the nit-picking objections his own people kept raising in discussions. A brief phone call led to a face-to-face meeting and the boxers agreed terms in quick time.

The bout was set for November 8, 2008, at Madison Square Garden, allowing Joe to fulfil another ambition in appearing at the historic New York arena. There was again a first-round knockdown for Calzaghe to overcome, but from the next session until the last the Welshman turned on a magnificent display against one of the best of his era; all three judges gave Joe every round except the opener.

Joe celebrates another win with sons Connor and Joe, Jr, who is now a promising amateur himself

Enzo regarded it as the best performance of his son's career, but Joe had already decided it would be his last hurrah. He had lost the hunger and called it a day after 46 straight victories. There was a doomed attempt at promoting, while an appearance on *Strictly Come Dancing* was no more successful.

But his place in sporting history is secure. One of only two people elected to the Welsh Sports Hall of Fame while still active – Paralympian legend Tanni Grey-Thompson is the other – Calzaghe was inducted into the International Boxing Hall of Fame in his first year of eligibility. Already an MBE – Enzo had one as well – he was upgraded to CBE, while locally he was made a Freeman of Caerphilly, while a new footbridge in his home town was named after Joe and his father.

The honours, parochial and worldwide, underline his position as one of the greatest sportsmen Wales has ever produced.

LEE CHURCHER
(1980-)

🏴 **Welsh Middleweight Champion 2012**

People always talk about "a puncher's chance". Maybe the other guy has all the skill, they say, but one fist in the right place can make that irrelevant. The former soldier from the Ringland estate proved the truth of the old adage.

Talented Rhondda southpaw Barrie Jones had been due to defend his Welsh light-middle title at the Newport Centre on May 19, 2012, but challenger Churcher struggled to make the weight and, with no reigning champion at middleweight, it was agreed to contest that belt instead.

Jones was not bothered. His right lead and supplementary left hook saw him dominate for eight and a half rounds, the well supported local man

Lee Churcher

unable to get inside. Then came the game-changer. One thunderous right sent Barrie crashing to the canvas and although he somehow made it to his feet, his glazed eyes prompted referee Wynford Jones to wave his arms. 'Lights Out' Lee had finally lived up to his name.

Churcher had boxed as a teenager, reaching a Welsh youth final, but rugby took over his affections for 10 years until he returned to the St Joseph's gym and gave the ring another go. After losing to Swansea gym owner Chris Ware in the Welsh ABA light-heavy final, he turned pro with Chris Sanigar.

There was a shocking early setback when winless Devonian Gavin Brook stopped him inside a round, while Aberystwyth's heavier Jamie Ambler outscored him, but Lee was still matched with Bargoed's Gary Cooper for the vacant Welsh middle throne on home ground on May 7, 2011.

It ended in confusion and injustice. Churcher pulled out at the end of the fifth, claiming a damaged hand; referee Roddy Evans, misunderstanding the new rule regarding accidental injury, intended to apply to cut eyes, ruled a Technical Draw as the pair were level after four. Gary should have won on a retirement – and, had the new law indeed applied, the fifth, clearly won by Cooper, should have been scored, giving him victory by that route as well.

None of this was Churcher's fault and four wins in five bouts earned him the shot at Jones which was to see him crowned. But then his world turned upside down. He admitted a charge of conspiracy to supply cocaine and was sentenced to four years in jail.

When he was released on parole after serving 21 months, he wanted to resume his career, but the Board's policy at the time insisted that former prisoners had to wait for their full term to be complete before their licences could be returned. Already 34, Lee had no time to wait, so he linked up with the Malta Boxing Commission, who had begun to promote on British soil and featured several fighters outlawed by the domestic authorities.

There were a few contests, all wins, among the broken promises and cancelled shows, but also the inescapable knowledge that the real stuff was happening elsewhere. So once he had completed his four-year exile, Churcher applied for the restoration of his licence and was welcomed back into sporting respectability early in 2017.

NATHAN CLEVERLY
(1987-)

🥊 **WBO Light-Heavyweight Champion 2011-13**

🥊 **WBA Light-Heavyweight Champion 2016-17**

🥊 **European Light-Heavyweight Champion 2010**

🥊 **Commonwealth Light-Heavyweight Champion 2008-10**

🥊 **British Light-Heavyweight Champion 2009-11**

🥊 **WBA Inter-Continental Cruiserweight Champion 2014**

The man from ITV Wales set up his camera at the back of the lecture theatre in Cardiff University's maths department. His colleague asked the students to let one of their number sit in a central position. They obliged readily enough, but with an air of bewilderment. Why were the television people so interested in this guy?

He may have been an anonymous undergraduate at the time, but a week later Nathan Cleverly was Commonwealth light-heavyweight champion. And he went on to become Wales's first official two-time world titleholder – not to mention earning an honours degree.

It was the success of a family acquaintance that began everything for the lad from Phillipstown. "I was 10 and wanted to be a footballer," recalls Nathan, "I used to get into street fights, but my mother was dead against me taking up boxing."

His father, singer Vince, had known Enzo Calzaghe since the Sardinian joined his band as a stand-in lead guitarist for a week-long gig in Barry Island. And that made all the difference.

"Mum read on teletext that Dad's friend's son had won a world title," says Nathan, "and she let him take me down to meet Enzo. That's where it all started."

There followed a selection of age-group honours, including a gold in the Four Nations juniors, before the youngster, now living in Cefn Fforest, joined the pro ranks while still a teenager. Manager Frank Warren kept him busy, frequently on Joe Calzaghe undercards, and the bill-topper was one of a small band still in Manchester's MEN Arena at midnight to watch him halt unbeaten Tony Quigley, a win which prompted little Enzo to claim that Cleverly, not the highly hyped Amir Khan, was the best 19-year-old in Britain.

His apprenticeship continued with success in Las Vegas on the Calzaghe-Bernard Hopkins show before 'Clev' widely outpointed former holder Tony Oakey at the Everton Park Sports Centre, Liverpool, on October 10, 2008, to claim the vacant Commonwealth light-heavy crown. He defended it three times before adding the British title, acquired with a seventh-round stoppage of unbeaten East

Nathan and Vince show off his four belts

Anglian Danny McIntosh at York Hall on July 18, 2009 – the same night the aforementioned Khan won his first world belt – before retaining both honours against former Olympian Courtney Fry.

This success came despite upheaval behind the scenes. A major row had seen the Calzaghes split with Warren, leaving Nathan with a choice to make: did he stay with his Sardinian mentor and break with the country's top promoter or remain with Warren and seek a new trainer? He opted to stick with Warren and father Vince took over in the corner and the gym.

It all seemed to be working as 'Clev' extended his collection to include the vacant European championship, collected at Wembley Arena on February 13, 2010, with a five-round demolition of Italian Antonio Brancalion. Unbeaten German-Armenian Karo Murat was seen off in an

official WBO eliminator and attention turned to the holder, Jürgen Brähmer, a former world junior gold medallist whose amateur record included a one-round win over Ricky Hatton. But Brähmer was notoriously reluctant to leave his native Germany, while recurrent problems with the law also restricted his movements.

His inactivity led the WBO to match Cleverly and Alejandro Lakatos for the interim strap, but the Romanian-born Spaniard withdrew with injury – in fact,

Cleverly (left) sees off Courtney Fry

he never boxed again – and was replaced at short notice by awkward French spoiler Nadjib Mohammedi. Having seen just one short clip on YouTube, Nathan took no risks en route to a unanimous decision in Dave Parris's last fight as a referee.

Finally, it seemed Brähmer was ready to rock and roll and the showdown was set for May 21, 2011, at the O2. But once again Jürgen was a no-show and this time the WBO ran out of patience, stripping him and upgrading the Welshman to full champion. There was still a TV date to save and – after a vocal intervention by Tony Bellew, then forced to admit he could not make the weight in time – Pole Aleksy Kuziemski was called in for what was now a title defence.

Cleverly, frustrated at the anti-climactic way in which he had achieved his dream, battered the outgunned, outskilled substitute, whose face was a bloody mess when American referee Mark Nelson called a halt in the fourth. Next up was the noisy Bellew, accommodated before his own screaming supporters at Liverpool's Echo Arena.

After a fractious build-up – police were called to a Cardiff hotel following post-press conference exchanges between Vince and one of Bellew's crew – the atmosphere was hostile, but Nathan maintained control of his emotions and his boxing to take what seemed a clear-cut decision, although judge Terry O'Connor's strange 114-114 card denied him a unanimous victory. Bellew was later to claim robbery, but his body language at the final bell suggested he knew the truth.

Unambitious American southpaw Tommy Karpency lost every round in Cardiff in a fight remembered more for the presence at ringside of another Welsh maths ace, Carol Vorderman, while a profile-raising trip to Los Angeles saw 'Clev' accompanied to the ring by Tom Jones and Mickey Rourke before he saw off late sub Shawn Hawk in the eighth.

The plan was that it would pave the way for an encounter with the legendary Bernard Hopkins, but first Nathan had to accommodate his mandatory challenger, German-Kosovan Robin Krasniqi, who won just

Mickey Rourke and Tom Jones with 'Clev' in LA

one round on the three cards. Next up was a much tougher task.

Sergey Kovalev, a decorated amateur in Russia, had moved to Florida to turn pro. Not until his tenth fight did he find an opponent to take him beyond two rounds and he had halted 19 men in a 22-bout rampage interrupted only by a Technical Draw following a head clash. Trained by former world champion John David Jackson, he arrived at the Motorpoint Arena on August 17, 2013, with mayhem in mind.

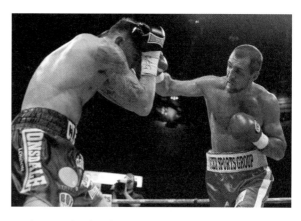

Nathan under fire from Kovalev

It proved an experience as educational for Cleverly as any at university. He managed to cut Kovalev near the right eye in the second, but the third saw the boom come down. A big right, a left uppercut and a volley of left hooks rocked the champion, before another right dropped him to one knee.

Nathan tried to hold, but 'Krusher' shook him free and battered him to the canvas once more. Terry O'Connor was close to stepping in, but the bell rang and the moment had passed. It was only postponed, however: when Cleverly, still dazed, came under fire again the burly Brummie referee called a halt after just 29 seconds of the fourth.

As so often with boxers after a first defeat, Nathan, after taking a few months to decide if he wanted to continue boxing, opted for changes all round. He moved up to cruiserweight, switched promoters to Matchroom and looked for a new trainer to replace his father. He spent a month in London, working with David Haye's mentor, Adam Booth, but while he enjoyed the gym work he was less enamoured with life in the Smoke. Instead he turned to the man who had been his conditioning coach for the last few years, Darren Wilson.

And Wilson deserves much credit for bringing Nathan up to the new weight – cruiser is 25lb above light-heavy, easily the biggest gap in the sport – so successfully that there was barely an ounce of surplus flesh when he took the scales in the Queen Street sun before his comeback against Trinidadian Shawn Corbin.

After one round's exploratory activity, Cleverly upped the pace in the second, rocking Corbin with right uppercuts and battering him in his own corner until Richie Davies stepped between them. Shawn's extrovert manager, Lystra Dogboe, made her dissatsfaction known, but there was only relief on the face of her boxer. Meanwhile, one ringside observer leapt in the air with joy. For Tony Bellew, a lucrative rematch was one step closer.

Matchroom boss Eddie Hearn promptly put the pair together on a bill in Liverpool, each facing eminently beatable South American opponents. 'Clev' fulfilled his part admirably, flooring Argentine champion Alejandro Valori with a vicious left to the body in the second and it was a credit to the visitor's will-power that he survived a few more before being dropped again and stopped with a repeat shot in the fourth.

Nathan was in a ringside seat by the time Bellew uncorked a superb left to spark Brazilian Julio Cesar dos Santos in the fifth, but only after shipping a series of rights to his unprotected jaw. Tony, still pumped up, strode to the ropes to unleash a volley at the Welsh observer and when Sky brought them together for a marginally more formal exchange, piled on the vitriol. Cleverly, more controlled, responded in kind, but gave the impression he was playing a marketing role, whereas Bellew's diatribe contained real venom.

One of the Scouser's main lines of argument was that he was no longer "a 175" and that the step up to cruiser had made him a much more formidable foe. When they met again at the Echo Arena, the truth of his claim was obvious. Bellew, a heavyweight in his amateur days, put on a stone between weigh-in and fight time; Nathan added a single pound. The difference proved telling.

The first six rounds saw the Welshman circling the ring, firing in the left jab, and blocking or evading Bellew's offerings. Even damage to his right hand, caused when he landed a blow to Tony's forehead in the third, did not unduly alter matters. But around the halfway stage Cleverly began to slow, taking breaks on the ropes, and the last few sessions largely consisted of the local man hurling punches at an immobile opponent. Most were blocked, but many landed. When the first score announced favoured Cleverly by a single point, even he was surprised. The other two judges preferred Bellew by two and four points. Justice was done.

"Trying to box with that extra weight uses up a lot of energy and it's something I'm not used to," said Nathan afterwards. "My speed was OK, but you pay the price in the later rounds."

The move back to light-heavy was inevitable. With Hearn working closely with the Sauerlands, promoters of the formerly reluctant Brähmer, now WBA champion, a title shot was soon pencilled in for Cleverly. There was the formality of proving he could make the weight – achieved via a 24-second blitz of hapless Czech Tomas Man at the O2 – and Nathan was invited to Germany. But there were strings attached: if he won, he would be bound to the Sauerland Brothers for his next fights. And when

Al Haymon, the new force on the American scene, came calling, he found receptive ears.

Brähmer was snubbed and the Welshman headed for Chicago to face locally based Andrzej Fonfara for the WBC International belt the Pole had earned by stopping Julio César Chávez, Jr, one of four world champions he had beaten. It would pay well, while victory could earn Nathan further big purses and a possible shot at WBC boss Adonis Stevenson, who had been held to points by the tough Fonfara. But it was a big ask.

Yet the first third of the bout saw Cleverly displaying the greater variety and volume of blows, if occasionally worryingly open to crowd favourite Andrzej's left hooks. By the fifth, Nathan was confident enough to showboat, whooping and hurling shots from around his waist. But two rounds later everything changed.

Suddenly the visitor was covering his face as Fonfara rained in blows. His nose was shattered, while there was further pain from a left ear which swelled ominously. From that point on, although 'Clev' kept firing, most of the ordnance was incoming and the hometown hero had established a clear advantage by the end of a contest which set a record for the most punches thrown by two light-heavies in a bout monitored by the CompuBox stats firm.

It was nearly a year before Nathan reappeared, but there was no easy warm-up opponent. Instead, the Welshman travelled to Germany, finally to face Brähmer on October 1, 2016, at the Jahnsportforum, just outside the walls of the medieval town of Neubrandenburg, north of Berlin.

At first Cleverly's left lead and the champion's southpaw equivalent seemed to cancel each other out, but by the second Nathan was setting a fast pace, hoping that Jürgen, four days shy of his 38th birthday, would tire. Working so much at close quarters left the visitor open to left hooks, with Brähmer happy to oblige.

By the sixth it seemed the challenger's body punches were having an effect. It was nevertheless a shock when the holder left his stool seconds before the bell to start the seventh and walked across the ring to inform the Welshman that he was handing

Cleverly celebrates becoming a two-time champion

over his title. An injury sustained in the fourth had hampered the use of his right hand, and he explained that, while he could have continued, he wanted to prolong his career. Given his age and the fact that he was giving up the belt while two points ahead on all three cards, this reasoning seemed strange.

For Cleverly, there was only one explanation. "I broke his heart," said the man who had just become Wales's first two-time world champion, to the wild enthusiasm of the handful of travelling supporters in a capacity 4,600 crowd. And the reluctance of his German rival – later diagnosed with a "minor muscle tear" in his forearm – to commit to a date for the rematch guaranteed by his contract seemed to support that hypothesis.

Brähmer's indecision meant it was 10 months before Nathan returned to the ring – and circumstances were a bit different from the tranquility of Neubrandenburg. He found himself on the Las Vegas Strip, staying in a hotel with its own rollercoaster rumbling past his window, ready to defend against former super-middle king Badou Jack, a Swede long based in 'Sin City', on the undercard of the hugely hyped showdown between all-time great Floyd Mayweather and UFC superstar Conor McGregor.

Cleverly matched Jack in a fast-paced opener, but the challenger, showing economy and accuracy of punch, was soon in command. When his nose 'went' in the third, the Welshman found himself up against it and by the end of the fourth trainer Lou del Valle was telling Badou, "He's done!"

That analysis was both succinct and faultless. Jack stepped up his assaults throughout the fifth and Cleverly, though still on his feet, was shipping heavy punishment on the ropes when referee Tony Weeks moved to the rescue. It proved to be the last act in a glittering career.

The dethroned monarch took to Twitter to announce his retirement, admitting there were "too many miles on the clock". But it had been an incredible journey.

DENYS CRONIN
(1962-)

🥊 **Welsh Middleweight Champion 1987-91**

When 11-year-old Denys Cronin first laced up the gloves at Senghenydd ABC, he made an immediate impact, stopping his first three rivals. But he wanted more. So he transferred to the Llanbradach gym where he hoped former Empire Games medallist Don Braithwaite would add a little polish to his power.

It worked. The Aber Valley lad – one of eight children of an Irish father, himself the eldest of 18 – went on to join that select group who have claimed Welsh titles in both amateur and professional codes.

He won two Welsh ABA championships and one British. After a controversial points loss to future Olympian Brian Schumacher, Cronin made no mistake the following year, battering Scot Alex McCulloch to a third-round defeat.

His crowd-pleasing quality prompted a feeding frenzy among the professional managers and Frank Warren emerged with the sought-after signature. His new boss gave him a home debut at Cardiff's STAR Centre, but lanky Midlander Gary Tomlinson outjabbed him and took the verdict.

Clearly, for all the hard work put in by Braithwaite and, later, by Dai Gardiner, the stocky Cronin was likely to find points decisions hard to come by. The answer was to take such matters out of the equation – so he proceeded to stop his next seven opponents.

The run included a clash at the Newport Centre on January 20, 1987, for the vacant Welsh middleweight throne. The other corner held West Walian Steve Davies, the light-middle champion, stepping up a division. Bad weather had meant Cronin doing his "roadwork" on an exercise bike, but fitness never became an issue as Davies's gamble backfired spectacularly.

Within the first round the Pembroke Dock boxer dropped to one knee in delayed response to a left to the temple; an uppercut had him hanging on

Denys Cronin

Cronin has Chris Eubank covering up

at the bell. Denys, who had now moved house the short distance from Senghenydd to Abertridwr, ignored Steve's attempts to hold him off, brushing aside the lighter man's punches to floor him once more with a right which actually lifted its recipient off the canvas.

Ivor Bassett, the Rhondda official who had voted against Cronin in his debut, looked long into Davies's eyes before letting him continue. Despite bravely trying to respond, Steve was back on the deck from a sweeping left hook in the second. He rose at nine, but this time it was all over.

There were to be few other victory celebrations. Twice Cronin lost to a young black fighter Brendan Ingle had whimsically dubbed Slugger O'Toole – apparently the lad's real name, Fidel Castro Smith, was not distinctive enough! A trip to Italy brought a two-round blitz by future European champion Francesco dell'Aquila, along with a split from Warren.

Denys claimed the only points win of his career, flooring unbeaten Irish champion Ray Close twice in a bout cut to four rounds for TV requirements. Close went on to draw in a world title challenge to Chris Eubank – and the 'Brighton Braggart' was next in line for Cronin, following his trademark vault over the STAR Centre ropes by strutting to his 20th straight victory in three rounds.

Close gained revenge in Belfast on St Patrick's Day, while a visit to Holland ended with veteran Alex Blanchard – he had lost his European light-heavy belt to Yorkshireman Tom Collins at Savva's nightclub, near Usk – hammering Denys into retirement after six painful sessions.

The Welshman took more than a year out, looking after his four children while his wife was in hospital, but returned with one of the best performances of his career. Yet it was to be his swansong.

He travelled to Leeds to face Cardiff-born local Michael Gale, whose 100 per cent record was ended by a draw after eight closely contested rounds. The pair were rewarded with a smattering of coins and notes thrown in by ringsiders, but, while Gale went on to contest the Commonwealth throne, Cronin never boxed again. He had suffered a torn retina during the bout which left him blind in the right eye. Surgery restored his sight, but it meant an end to his career.

FREDDIE CROSS
(1935-)

Welsh Middleweight Champion 1957

British Middleweight Contender 1958

They may not have been totally serious, but *Boxing News* had a point. As soon as he heard that Freddie Cross was turning professional, the trade paper's gossip columnist suggested that he might as well put in a claim for the Welsh middleweight title.

The de facto champion, Roy Agland, had not boxed for more than a year and, although he insisted he had not retired, never did return to the ring. And there were precious few would-be challengers to force the authorities' hand.

Serving in the RAF at the time, Cross was unfortunate to be competing directly with one of Britain's top amateurs, Bruce Wells. He still managed to pick up a record four national sea cadet titles and represented both Wales and the ABA – in effect, Britain.

Once back in civvy street, he turned pro with Tommy Daly, a former London docker, who found him a job as a lorry driver, based in Bermondsey, where he trained with Toby Noble. His enthusiastic following – from Nuneaton, where he grew up, as well as London – were able to cheer victories in his first 11 bouts, including a decision over Swansea stylist Teddy Barrow in a thriller at Streatham Ice Rink, where ringsiders included former world welter ruler Kid Gavilán; the 'Cuban Hawk' pronounced Cross a future champion. The admiration was mutual: Freddie sparred with Gavilán and regards it as the highlight of his career. "I learned so much from him," he says.

Freddie Cross

Cross (left) tangles with rival Phil Edwards

With Agland having finally vacated the Welsh throne, the area council opted for a rematch with Barrow to decide his successor. It was Freddie's first ring appearance in his native land when the pair touched gloves at Sophia Gardens Pavilion on January 16, 1957. It was actually familiar territory for manager Daly, who was posted to Cardiff for four years during the war.

Freddie's family moved from his native Abertillery when he was four and he returned to Wales with a strong Midlands accent. Barrow had the greater experience, but Cross countered well to the body when Teddy moved in. In a thrilling bout, Freddie seemed always to have the edge, despite a seventh-round rally from the Swansea man which forced him to retreat.

It looked certain to go the distance, but lightning struck in the 11th. Cross found a short right which dropped his rival, who rose too soon. Freddie showed great coolness, picking his punches calmly and flooring Barrow twice more before North Walian referee Billy Jones stepped in and pronounced him the new champion of the nation he left as a child.

Cross's winning streak ended with a cuts loss, but he was back on track before defending against Cardiffian Phil Edwards on August 21, 1957, outdoors at Pandy Park, Cross Keys, where the Gwent valley fans proved a little excitable. When referee Joe Morgan gave the verdict to his fellow-townsman, chairs were among the missiles hurled towards the ring and one disgruntled supporter went so far as to kick Edwards's manager, Benny Jacobs, in the groin as he tried to protect his boxer. Did they have a case for complaint?

It seemed that way. Cross's stiff left lead earned him the early sessions, his neat footwork keeping him clear of most of the challenger's hooks, even if one brought blood from Freddie's right eyebrow in the fourth. Phil took the fifth, but the Abertillery fighter excelled in the seventh, before having to take a knee in the next. Despite a strong finish by the Cardiffian, few neutral observers thought he had done enough.

The Welsh Area Council ordered a rematch, but Edwards needed surgery on his nose and Cross passed the time by tackling future world champion Terry Downes. Better than that, he actually beat him, though it was thanks to a gashed eyebrow.

A 3,000 capacity crowd at Sophia Gardens Pavilion on April 23, 1958, saw Edwards leave no room for doubt second time around in a bout also recognised as a British title eliminator. Hundreds of fans unable to gain admission were given running commentaries by policemen and stewards as the local man forced Freddie into immediate retreat.

Phil focussed on the body, leaving angry red welts on the challenger's ribs. Cross then picked up damage next to both eyes, the left accompanied by a swelling which left him almost blind by the end, when London referee Bill Williams raised Edwards's arm.

Freddie was matched with former light-heavy ruler Alex Buxton in another eliminator and jabbed his way to a clear decision over the Watford man, 11 years older. A final hurdle awaited against John 'Cowboy' McCormack, but each was injured and the bout never happened before the Welshman headed Down Under to fulfil a contract there.

It was not a successful venture, Freddie being stopped three times, although a trip across the Tasman brought some joy, with a decision over former New Zealand welter king Billy Beazley. Cross did not box again for five years.

When he returned in 1964 it was at light-heavy, where his only loss in six contests came on points against recent British titleholder Chic Calderwood. But when Guyanese former victim Clarence Prince halted him in six, it spelt the end for Freddie. Surgery on his troublesome right mitt had not solved the problem and he felt there was little point in continuing.

Once his career was over, Cross returned to Nuneaton, where – apart from a five-year period running a Blackpool hotel – he has lived ever since.

MORGAN CROWTHER
(1869-1932)

World Bantamweight Challenger 1890

Nobody could accuse Morgan Crowther of having a boring life. A hard-drinking, hard-fighting youngster, his name was mentioned – unflatteringly – in the House of Commons and he survived a stabbing before becoming a wealthy man and mingling with politicians and power-brokers.

Originally from Abercarn, he was living in Newport when he first caught the public eye. Billy Leahy, who owned an oyster bar in the town, staged tournaments upstairs involving the local youth. Crowther impressed and Leahy began to guide his career, in partnership with veteran Cardiff bookie Billy Morgan.

There were few able to match him "in the old style" as, despite lacking punching power, he made up for it with an incredible ability to absorb punishment, frequently outlasting better men. With the gloves on, he did conjure up a knockout to claim his first title, flattening Jack Hicks in Cheltenham in a bout billed for the West of England 118lb championship.

Morgan Crowther

A more notable name was added to the Crowther record when he took on Brummie Nunc Wallace, later to face American hall-of-famer George Dixon for a world belt. Morgan seemed to have taken control by the fifth, when a Wallace supporter, worried about his wager, climbed through the ropes and refused to leave. The referee abandoned the contest and later awarded it to the Welshman on a disqualification.

Crowther promptly challenged all and sundry at 8st 8lbs – titles were disputed at two-pound intervals and the term "bantamweight" had not been generally adopted – and found himself up against Londoner 'Mighty' Bill Baxter on January

27, 1890, at the Kennington Social Club, with world and "English" honours at stake.

Morgan in respectable later life

Baxter's left soon had him bleeding profusely from the mouth and at one stage, Crowther's handlers objected that Bill's left glove had become so saturated with their man's gore that it now weighed more than the agreed amount; it was duly changed for a fresh weapon. Little altered, however, in the flow of the fight (or the blood) and the 17th round saw the towel float in from the Welsh corner. Morgan was not the only loser on the night. Many of the posher punters were seated in a loft, with the trapdoor closed once they had climbed the ladder. Several local ne'er-do-wells had entered with them and, in sweltering heat, proceeded to remove everything of value down to the last brass collar stud.

Boxing was still a sport at the limits of legality. Morgan's regular clashes with Bristolian 'Chaffy' Hayman seemed to provoke particular interest from the authorities. After a set-to near Worcester, each man was jailed for a month, while a later meeting in Bath saw them fined £25 and bound over to keep the peace.

Two significant collisions in Kennington with Londoner Arthur Wilkinson bookended 1891. Both, though with gloves, were billed as fights to the finish, but when the first was still going at 1 a.m. the police called a halt after 45 rounds. No decision was given, but Wilkinson conceded victory to the Welshman for threequarters of the £100 purse. The rematch, this time for £200 and the British championship at 8st 8lbs, saw Morgan gain a more orthodox triumph, forcing Arthur to quit in the 42nd session.

Another trip to Kennington, however, ended painfully for Crowther, who was knocked out by a right from Leicester's Tom Wilson, but the stocky Gwent fighter reversed his fortune when he dropped Hackney's Fred Johnson for the full count in the last of a 20-rounder at Shoreditch; some retrospectively claimed that the 8st 12lbs title had been at stake, though that was never mentioned at the time.

A few months later, in June 1893, Morgan, now married to the daughter of a Cardiff publican, was given a temporary licence to run the Moulders Arms on Newport's Marshes Road, but his reputation outside the ropes prompted Cumbrian MP Sir Wilfrid Lawson to ask the Home Secretary whether this was a suitable person for the post. Herbert Asquith, 15 years before becoming Prime Minister, suggested that when they reviewed the matter the justices would act "in the interests of the community". Sensing which way the wind was blowing, Crowther dropped the idea.

His ring exploits were now confined to exhibitions and music hall appearances, but there was one last hurrah. It came before the bow-tie brigade at the National Sporting Club on March 29, 1897, with Londoner Dave Wallace on the other stool. Only Morgan's renowned resilience saw him through the scheduled 20 rounds, and top referee Bernard Angle's verdict was a formality.

Crowther became a commission agent – a bookie to you and me – travelling widely from his home at the appropriately named Ascot House in Cardiff's Lansdowne Road, while he was also a director of the Badminton Club, an enthusiastic member of Canton Conservative Club and a supporter of local charities.

Not that he was universally popular: one acquaintance, Charlie Thomas, stabbed him in the abdomen, piercing the liver, after Morgan had apparently been to Charlie's house while he was away and tried it on with his wife. Thomas was acquitted of attempted murder, but was jailed for three years for wounding with intent. During the trial, it emerged that Crowther had two convictions for assaulting the police and one for defrauding a railway company, as well as those for prizefighting.

But they were in the past. Morgan died at home, aged 63, following an operation and was buried in the grounds of Llandaff Cathedral, underlining his progress from reprobate to respectable citizen.

BILLY DAVIES
(1922-1985)

🐾 Welsh Flyweight Champion 1947-48

In Wales, it is not so remarkable that two boxers named Billy Davies have been national flyweight champion. The first, from Cardiff, reigned way back in 1918, but was still serving the sport as secretary of the Welsh Area Council when his Nantyglo namesake claimed the same title three decades later.

William Henry, to give the latter his full handle – followed big brother Tommy into the ring, differentiated from other Davieses by the nickname 'Dingle' after their father, who came from that part of Blaina.

Tommy's chance at Welsh honours came at featherweight in 1944, but he was outpointed by Llanharan's Syd Worgan at Newport Athletic Ground. At that stage, Billy had just lost his unbeaten record to Lancastrian Teddy Gallagher. But a string of victories convinced the Welsh authorities to match the younger Davies with Maldwyn Baker, from Aberbargoed, in an eliminator for the flyweight crown relinquished by Swansea's Jackie Kiley.

It meant a return to Rodney Parade for the Davies clan and Billy exorcised the memory of Tommy's defeat, flooring Baker repeatedly and raising a grotesque swelling on his left ear. When a right swing burst the balloon in the seventh, blood flowed as if a tap had been turned on. With their man way behind, Maldwyn's corner pulled him out at the bell.

Billy then spoiled the debut of Tiryberth youngster Haydn Jones, later to reign over Wales's featherweights, and manager Billy Hughes began to challenge all and sundry. He bit off more than his man could chew when he took him to London to face highly rated prospect Terry Allen. Davies earned respect for his gameness, but the outstanding Islington fighter won inside four rounds, another step on his march to world domination.

Then Billy was stopped in one, on cuts, by future European ruler Dickie O'Sullivan, while he was also

Billy Davies

knocked out in four by former Welsh No 1 Ronnie Bishop. Perhaps the fact that the bout took place in Barrow meant it escaped the attention of the powers-that-be; whatever, Davies was still permitted to take on Gilbert Hughes, from Merthyr, for the vacant title.

Their clash on April 21, 1947, was the first championship bout ever staged at Neath's Gwyn Hall, where more than 1,200 watched a one-sided affair. Davies's left was constantly in Hughes's face and by the sixth Gilbert was cut over an eye and bleeding steadily from the nose. Billy reverted to long-range work and was in total control when referee C.B. Thomas called a halt in the 11th. Hughes looked astonished, but Thomas explained, via the MC, that he was so far behind that he could not have won even if he had gone on.

Davies celebrated by overcoming former conqueror Gallagher, but his form took a downturn and he was deposed as champion at the Market Hall, Pontypool, on June 14, 1948, with Cardiffian George Sutton on the opposite stool. Sutton had won a British schoolboy title back before the war, but was a surprising choice to have a straight shot at the title, given that he had lost all three pro bouts – one when he was knocked out while hitching up his shorts!

But George's first victory earned him a belt, although the decision left many ringsiders open-mouthed. Billy forced the pace throughout, with the challenger focussed on slipping the incoming left lead and responding with carefully chosen punches of his own. What he did was commendable, but few agreed with the referee that it had been enough.

Welsh bantam champion Norman Lewis had hopes of adding a second title, but the authorities would not recognise his meeting with Billy as an eliminator; just as well for the Nantyglo man, who was stopped in seven. Lewis duly deposed Sutton and Davies found himself facing George a year later for the right to challenge. The Cardiff man had not won since beating Billy 16 months earlier, but he managed to do it again in a close encounter.

That was enough for Davies. Brother Tommy had packed it in a month previously and Billy followed suit.

RON 'PONTY' DAVIES
(1937-)

European Bronze Medallist 1957

The switch-hitting southpaw from Llanbradach was one of the biggest enigmas in Welsh boxing. Had he put half the effort into training that he put into having a good time, there was no limit to what he might have achieved.

Many respected observers forecast great things for the young pitman as he excelled as an amateur. After becoming Welsh ABA flyweight champion on a walkover in 1955, he received his call-up papers and boxed for the next two years as a serviceman. That route took him all the way to a British ABA title in 1957.

Wales claimed they had no money to send anyone to that year's Europeans in Prague, a stance which drew a few acid comments in *Boxing News*. At the last minute, they changed their minds, selecting Davies, but still could not pay for a cornerman; the English generously took the lone Taff into their care.

Irish rival John Caldwell – a future pro world champion – had already been controversially eliminated before 'Ponty' took a 3-2 points decision over rugged Pole Henryk Kukier, who had won the competition four years previously. The performance delighted the watching Wales football squad, who, despite losing to the Czechs the next day, were on the way to qualifying for the following year's World Cup finals.

Next up was local hero Zdenek Petrina, who was jabbed and countered to a unanimous defeat even the partisan crowd accepted with good grace. They were less content with the result in the semi-final, jeering the announcement that Davies

Ron 'Ponty' Davies

had lost to German southpaw Manfred Homberg, Caldwell's fortunate conqueror, by a majority decision.

Davies promptly turned pro with Cardiffian Benny Jacobs, claiming two stoppage wins in two weeks. But plans for another two bouts fell through when he was confined to barracks for overstaying his leave from the Welch Regiment.

It was 10 months before he next appeared in the ring. But he promptly halted three more foes, including former British title challenger Len 'Luggie' Reece, clubbed into retirement after seven rounds.

Next up was talented Indian Pancho Bhatachaji at Sophia Gardens, but once again 'Ponty' went AWOL. Four days before the show, Jacobs tracked him down to a Caerphilly pub, where he claimed to be drinking fruit juice. His manager admitted that, technically, cider could be so described, but with his boxer now over nine stone, the fight was off and promoter Stan Cottle, already ill in bed, felt infinitely worse. An initial ban was replaced by a £75 fine and the miscreant was allowed to box on, but it was 16 months before he was back.

An under-prepared Davies was blowing by halfway, but still outpointed Rotherham's all-action Eddie Barraclough in the Penydarren Park rain and Merthyr promoter Theo Davies opened talks with British fly king Frankie Jones, eventually tempting him to Ynys Park, Aberdare, for a non-title 10-rounder. It was a little classic, Ron pacing himself well, and at the finish North Walian official Billy Jones opted for the Welshman's aggression over the Scot's elegant left-hand work.

Bhatachaji, who could boast a knockout win over Jones, finally faced Davies at Sophia Gardens Pavilion and it was a cracker, 'Ponty' matching his man for skill and control as well as maintaining his usual high workrate. But in the seventh, a clash of heads left Pancho, already bleeding near both eyes, with another nasty gash and cornerman George Odwell pulled him out.

Mickey Duff, then matchmaker for Harry Levene, paired Davies and his ABA final victim, Chingford postman Derek Lloyd, in a British final eliminator. But 'Ponty' vanished from the gym again; a few days later the runaway was spotted in Bournemouth by a waitress from Caerphilly.

Davies was also being lined up for a £1,000 payday in Cardiff against former European champion Young Martín, while Jacobs was looking at a proposal to take him to fight in the US. But the most exciting Welsh fighter of his generation never boxed again.

TONY DAVIES
(1952-)

- Welsh Bantamweight Champion 1973-74
- British Flyweight Challenger 1974
- Commonwealth Games Silver Medallist 1970

One wasted talent in a family is more than enough. Yet the younger brothers of Ron 'Ponty' Davies fell for the same temptations and ended their careers similarly unfulfilled. Gary had three wins and then vanished, while Tony managed to claim a few honours in a career that nevertheless promised more.

The youngest of 10, his natural ability was so obvious as an 11-year-old that trainer Don Braithwaite gave him his first contest just three days after he first appeared at the Wingfield Hotel gym. His tiny frame meant a scarcity of opponents, but he was fortunate that a light-flyweight class had just been introduced at the Commonwealth Games and the Welsh selectors duly picked him.

Davies arrived in Edinburgh aiming to improve on the bronze medal won in Cardiff 12 years earlier by trainer Braithwaite. He succeeded in style. A bye in the sparsely populated new division meant a single victory would guarantee a prize, but 'Umper' – as he was always known – needed a 3-2 verdict to get past fellow-teenager Blackson Mazyopa, from Zambia, after a spirited tussle. The semi-final saw him climb from his sick bed to outscore Australian southpaw Peter Butterfield, but the throat infection took its toll when he faced Ugandan prison officer James Odwori to decide the gold, all five judges favouring the tall African.

The horse-loving Llanbradach lad harboured dreams of becoming a jockey, but instead enlisted in the Royal Regiment of Wales in the hope of finding more ring action. After he flattened the Army champion twice in a few weeks, nobody else wanted to know and Tony bought himself out of the service for £25, turning pro with brother Ron's long-suffering manager, Benny Jacobs.

Tony Davies (right) sees off Aussie Peter Butterfield to reach the Commonwealth Games final

Tony Davies (right) with trainer Don Braithwaite

Opening with a one-round victory, Davies won his first five before being matched with Cardiffian Joey Deriu for the Welsh bantam throne vacated by Tonyrefail's Colin Miles. A shot at John McCluskey's British fly belt was promised, with the Scot ringside at Aberavon's Executive Hotel on September 12, 1973. He was witness to a near-tragedy.

In a gruelling contest, the crew-cut 'Umper', unsettled after being cut for the first time in the opener, slowly found his rhythm, but was shaken by successive rights in the sixth. The long-haired Deriu, too, stayed on his feet despite some heavy shots – until the bell rang to begin the 10th and last round. The 23-year-old rose from his stool, touched gloves with his opponent and collapsed. Referee Adrian Morgan waved a halt and Joey was rushed to Morriston Hospital, where he lay in a coma for several weeks before beginning a slow recovery.

The McCluskey plan went on the back burner. When Davies reappeared after eight months, it was to defend his bantam belt against Pontlottyn's Tony Williams, whose own career had included a five-year break after his hands were crushed in a road accident. Williams displayed some neat left-hand work, but shipped steady punishment and referee Jim Brimmell ended the affair midway through the sixth.

Promoter Eddie Richards turned his attention back to McCluskey and the match was made for the Top Rank on October 14, 1974. The Welsh Area Council demanded a check-weigh the week before and were gratified to discover that Tony was less than two pounds above the limit, despite scoffing a daily steak.

In fact, it was McCluskey who tipped the scales 10 ounces over, a surplus he shed with a little exercise in the Top Rank's boiler room. That took him longer than winning the fight. It was over in 125 seconds.

'Umper' had managed to land a couple of lefts to encourage his supporters, but McCluskey's movement meant there were no more. Instead the Hamilton man worked Davies's body before abruptly switching his attentions upstairs; three left hooks to the jaw, followed by a glancing right, sent the challenger to the canvas. He somehow scrambled up at nine, but was unable to ward off the hurricane and was promptly decked again. He rose at six, but on shaky legs, and referee Wally Thom spread his arms to end the slaughter.

The end - 'Umper' is demolished by British champion John McCluskey

Still only 22, Davies never boxed again. Whenever shows came to the Club Double Diamond, he would talk of packing in the beer and moving to Reading, where promoter Bev Walker promised to revive his career. He never made it across the bridge.

TONY DOHERTY
(1983-)

- Celtic Welterweight Champion 2005-07

- Welsh Welterweight Champion 2008-13

The traveller from Pontypool was not the first member of his family to achieve fame. His grandmother was in the Guinness Book of Records for having more than 500 grandchildren. And, at the age of 95, she made the trip from her London home to Widnes to watch Tony Doherty make his pro debut.

Given that she was accompanied by a hundred-odd relatives, including a week-old babe in arms, it is easy to see why promoters were so keen on the young welterweight. The fact that he had an immense amount of talent and a gift for excitement did his popularity no harm, either.

There was boxing in the blood. Limerick-born father Simon, the oldest of 22 children, had been a scrapper, and took seven-year-old Tony, the youngest of 17 – mother Margaret, from Tipperary, was also one of 17 – to St Joseph's ABC, Lewisham, but two years later the family moved to Wales and the nipper joined coach Tony Williams at the Pontypool and Panteg club. He proceeded to win no fewer than 11 age-group titles, captaining his new country at schools and youth level.

As a senior, he missed a sure-fire Commonwealth Games medal when an over-fussy doctor ruled him out for a minimal cut. That came between two Welsh ABA triumphs; following the second he signed for Frank Warren, migrating to Manchester to train with Brian Hughes, and made that winning bow at Widnes, outpointing veteran Karl Taylor – despite getting clipped as he looked down when wily opposing manager Nobby Nobbs told him his bootlaces were undone!

'The Doc' was carefully groomed, with former Commonwealth Games team-mate Taz Jones the first rival – in his 16th fight – with more wins than losses. He gained the verdict in the first Celtic title bout to be held in Wales, but few at Cardiff International Arena on September 10, 2005, agreed with Midlands referee

Tony Doherty

The final act - Doherty (left) loses to unsung Geraint Harvey

Lee Cook, who somehow gave the Cynon Valley fighter only two rounds in a tussle he controlled until the later stages.

Recurring hand injuries – including one, bizarrely caused as he tried to extract a tape from a video recorder, which cost him a bout against future world champion Kell Brook – interrupted Doherty's progress until a rematch with Jones at the Millennium Stadium. Driven by the memory of brother Francis, a victim of cystic fibrosis at 26, Tony started fast and steadily dismantled his man to earn a seventh-round stoppage. New mentor Jim McDonnell called him "technically the best I've ever trained" and claimed he could win a world title.

But his second Celtic defence, back at the CIA, saw the Pontypool boxer leading the complaints when Mickey Vann raised the arm of Scot Kevin McIntyre. For Doherty, who had to sweat off surplus pounds at the weigh-in, his first defeat also wrecked a planned British title eliminator.

He was inactive for eight months before returning to tackle Rhondda southpaw Barrie Jones for the vacant Welsh throne at the CIA on March 22, 2008. Tony, now back in Wales with Enzo Calzaghe, dominated a scrap marred by constant racist abuse from a group of Jones supporters undisturbed by smiling security staff. Barrie was bullied out of his elegant stride and, despite his late revival, referee Wynford Jones had Doherty three points up at the end.

The new Welsh champion demanded another crack at McIntyre, now wearing the Lonsdale Belt, but fate decreed differently. Kevin was stripped for failing to face the unbeaten Brook and when the Board sought someone to meet Kell for the vacant title, 'The Doc' was out of training and the chance went to the man he had just beaten, Jones.

Meanwhile, Doherty, whose fluctuating weight was frustrating Calzaghe, drifted out of the public eye – there were rumours of lucrative battles on the gipsy sites – and it was more than a year and a half before he reappeared in the officially sanctioned ring.

And it proved disastrous. The senior Calzaghe, dipping his toes in the world of promotion, needed Doherty's ticket-shifting presence and found him a "safe" opponent in Pontypridd light-middle Geraint Harvey, who had won just six of his 50 fights. Perhaps the effort of shedding five stone damaged Tony's punch resistance, but he was decked twice and stopped in three.

It was effectively the end of Doherty's formal career at just 26. He threatened a comeback with Gary Lockett, but it never materialised.

ROSIE ECCLES
(1996-)

🥊 **European Silver Medallist 2016**

Most girls who attend boxercise classes hope the workout will keep them in shape. Few enjoy the non-contact sessions so much that they want to try the real thing. 'Right-Hand Rose' was an exception.

A runner and swimmer until injury sidelined her for two years, her decision to change sports has paid off big-time. Eccles, from Chepstow, learned her craft at the local club and wore their colours in her first Welsh elite championships, in 2015, destroying Tredegar's Natasha Williams inside a round.

The useful England rep, Cherrelle Brown, outscored her in the final of the GB tournament, but the following year Rosie – having retained her national title on a walkover – turned silver into gold and gained revenge over Brown in the process, despite being floored for the first time. It was a measure of how quickly she was developing and there was further experience being collected at competitions abroad.

Eccles, now trained at Pontypool ABC by Mark and Lyndon James, was selected in a four-strong squad for the European championships in Bulgaria in November 2016. And while new clubmate Lauren Price struck bronze, the comparative novice went all the way to the light-welterweight final.

There was a clear-cut victory over Finn Anni Viantie, the Nordic champion, but Rosie had to settle for majority verdicts over world-ranked Italian Valentina Alberti and a tall and awkward Pole, Kinga Siwa. With the gold at stake, she found herself up against a familiar figure.

The Welsh girl had floored and outpointed Russian Alexandra Ordina the previous year in a multi-nations event, but this time things were different. Feeling less than 100 per cent, Eccles put up a good enough show to convince some observers that she had won – but the three judges favoured Ordina, a decision the loser agreed was correct.

Rosie Eccles

Rosie gains revenge over England's Cherrelle Brown to win the GB title

The truth about her infirmity only emerged after the Christmas break, when she was ill after a sparring session and was revealed as having suffered concussion. It meant a six-month lay-off, but as she returned to training there was good news on two fronts.

The same week as Rosie graduated with honours from Cardiff Metropolitan University – she now plans to study for a Masters degree in sports psychology – it was announced that two more weight divisions were to be added to the women's schedule at both Olympic and Commonwealth Games. One was welterweight, so the Monmouthshire girl moved up a division and set her sights on further honours to come.

MATTHEW EDMONDS
(1984-)

Commonwealth Bantamweight Challenger 2007

British Bantamweight Challenger 2009

A trip to any Weight Watchers class will provide ample evidence of how difficult it is to shift surplus pounds. How much harder must it be, then, to battle the scales against a deadline – and to do so at regular intervals. That was frequently the problem for the young window fabricator from Nash, on the edge of Newport.

The third of nine children – three of his six brothers boxed as amateurs – Matthew Edmonds first laced up the gloves at nine, when his father took him to the Torfaen Warriors gym. There followed Welsh and British success in various junior tournaments (he handed a first defeat to future world title challenger Kevin Mitchell on the way to one success) before he moved closer to home and the St Joseph's club in Newport.

Senior competition brought four Welsh championships, a Four Nations gold and appearances at a variety of international tournaments. They included two Commonwealth Games – beating future IBF champion Lee Selby in a box-off for selection in 2006 – each time going out to an eventual finalist. Following the second try, it was time to go pro, amateur mentor Tony Borg continuing as trainer, while Bristol-based Chris Sanigar held the managerial reins.

The first five contests were won without losing a round, but Scot Kris Hughes posed questions the Welshman could not solve. As a late substitute, a 5ft 11in southpaw was perhaps not the wisest choice! Ungainly and difficult to catch clean, Hughes did enough to edge a one-point victory over the frustrated local man.

Strange things happen in boxing, however, and promoter Frank Maloney, needing someone for Nottingham crowd-pleaser Jason Booth to face for the vacant Commonwealth bantam throne at Wigan's Robin Park Arena on December 8, 2007, chose Edmonds.

Matthew Edmonds

It was a big ask. Booth had worn IBO, British and Commonwealth belts in lighter divisions and his 32 bouts had included 11 scheduled for 12 rounds. Matty had no such experience to draw on. It did not show as he marched forwards in the early sessions, having the better of one or two, but eventually the Midlander's class began to tell. Right uppercuts jolted Edmonds's head back and as the Newport fighter moved into unfamiliar territory he began to tire. He was under steady fire late in the ninth and Marcus McDonnell eventually stepped between them.

Matty regrouped with a series of successes over imports from Africa and Eastern Europe and was rewarded with a chance at the British bantam crown, relinquished by new European king Ian Napa. The other corner at the atmospheric York Hall in London's East End on April 3, 2009 was occupied by Gary Davies, from St Helen's, who had earned his opportunity by stopping former holder Martin Power.

This time it was the Welshman's opponent who had never been beyond six and many pundits thought Edmonds could come on strong in the second half of the fight. Indeed, after Davies had forced him on to the back foot and built a substantial lead – one judge gave him every round – Matty rocked him with a solid left hook to open the seventh. But as he moved to follow up, he was caught by a right counter and floored.

With the assistance of the ropes, Edmonds clambered to his feet at four, still unsteady on his legs. Twice more he was bundled over – a count was given on one occasion – and when he dropped to his knees referee Dave Parris waved it off.

Eight months later Matty tried to re-establish his credentials against Davies victim Power in Newport, but it proved disastrous. Three times the Londoner decked him with counters and it was over in the fifth, the loser blaming weight-making for wrecking his punch resistance.

Similar troubles saw him shockingly stopped by Bradford journeyman Shaun Doherty; afterwards Edmonds admitted that he had piled on an incredible 18lb between the day-before weigh-in and the morning of fight day. Once again the strain of shedding it in the first place had left him vulnerable.

He took the hint, hanging up his gloves and turning to his other sporting love, running. While making a living as a carpenter, he won the Wales Marathon at his first attempt in 2012 and represented his country in France before surgery to remove a floating bone from an ankle left him sidelined for months.

Matty the marathon runner, finding success in a second sport

Other injuries have interrupted Matty's new career, but he is now back pounding the roads.

ARTHUR EVANS
(1885-1950)

Welsh Lightweight Champion 1914-15, 1915-22

If the talented Tirphil fighter had given up the day job and focussed on boxing he could have reached the very top. At least, so thought many respected observers of the time. But constant shiftwork down the pit meant lengthy periods of inactivity and interfered with the training necessary to succeed with his non-stop "hurricane style".

His early career has been lost in the mists of time, although he is thought to have been boxing for a good seven years before his first recorded scrap and was rated highly enough to have been offered trips to the US and New Zealand, each time opting to stay at home.

In the pre-Board era championships tended to have multiple claimants, but when Evans and another of the prime candidates met at Merthyr's Olympia Rink on August 2, 1913, the bout earned general recognition as the "resident champion", acknowledging Freddie Welsh's absence in the US. Caerau stylist Dai Roberts edged a decision disputed by most of the 4,000 crowd.

After a strange "knockout" victory over Liverpool's Jim Lloyd at Bargoed – the pair, in a clinch, fell from the ring in the second round, with Evans on top; Lloyd was unsconscious for 10 minutes and therefore counted out – Arthur went back to Merthyr for a final eliminator, only to lose on points to local Joe Johns.

Johns's challenge to Roberts ended in a No Contest, but the Caerau man – later to die in the war – relinquished his crown to move up in weight and Evans was matched with Johns to fill the vacancy. "Illness" (more likely a dispute over money) prompted Joe to withdraw and instead Arthur faced Cardiffian Billy McCarthy at Bargoed Pavilion on May 11, 1914. McCarthy was a three-time Welsh ABA champion, but making his paid debut; the gamble failed and Evans knocked him out in two.

Before Arthur could capitalise on his new status he suffered facial damage when a sports car in which he was travelling hit overhanging branches, but even when he was fit there were innumerable difficulties in agreeing terms with obvious challenger

Arthur Evans

Johns, the Merthyr man's recurrent rheumatism also complicating the issue. It was a year before they finally collided, on a military show at Cardiff Arms Park on May 22, 1915. Top London referee Eugene Corri headed west to officiate and he ruled, to some dissent among the 10,000 crowd, that Johns, now with the Royal Engineers, was the new Welsh champion.

Evans followed him into khaki and, with both stationed near Liverpool, it was on Merseyside that their third meeting took place just two months later. It was refereed by Newport's reigning British welter king, Johnny Basham, who soon warned Arthur for hitting on the break. Johns, despite a cut eye, floored Evans in the eighth. But the Tirphil man stormed back in a thrilling contest, dropping Joe at the end of the 16th and he was unable to come out for the next session. Evans had regained his title.

Arthur saw little ring activity over the next two years, but after an up-and-down draw with Ynysddu collier Billy Jones at Bargoed, a return was arranged with the belt apparently at stake. This time Evans climbed off the deck to take the decision, said to be his first points win in a 10-year career.

Dowlais boy Idris Jenkins twice outscored Arthur, but both bouts were over two-minute rounds and few gave much credence to his claims to the throne. When Evans vanished from the scene for the next two years, other boxers demanded title recognition, but when the Tirphil miner reappeared to face Blaenavon's Tommy Morgan at Blackwood Market Hall on March 20, 1922, it was treated as a defence. Now in his 39th year, Evans boxed surprisingly well early on, but gradually faded and began to come under steady pressure. He went down in the 10th and 11th, but referee Barnett stayed his hand until the towel came floating in.

The veteran, now living at New Tredegar, turned his attention to running a gym at the Tredegar Arms, where he passed on his ring wisdom to the next generation, including his sons, Young Arthur and Cliff.

CRAIG EVANS
(1989-)

- WBO European Lightweight Champion 2016-

- British Lightweight Challenger 2015

- European Schoolboys Bronze Medallist 2004

Boxing has seen some memorable trilogies over the years, with the third fight usually a decider after each fighter has won once. It is rare for it to follow two draws. That must make defeat in the final encounter all the harder to bear; thankfully, Craig Evans was the winner.

The youngster from Pontllanfraith began boxing at 10, following big brother Christian, later to blaze a trail in the bare-knuckle ranks; a third brother, Rhys, later had a brief pro career. Craig started at Fleur-de-Lys ABC, following trainer Alan Davies to Church Place – where Nathan Cleverly trained with his father, Vince – determined to follow in the footsteps of grandfather Selwyn, a Welsh champion in the 1950s. In the event, he surpassed that achievement, but it took time to get there.

Evans showed his promise with a European Schools bronze, before a senior career which brought Welsh honours and another bronze, at the EU championships, as well as the experience of going the distance with Ukrainian legend Vasyl Lomachenko. The pro scene beckoned.

Craig joined gym-mate Cleverly in the Frank Warren empire, but turned his back on home comforts to train in Manchester with Lee Beard. His debut victory, a 39-second demolition of Dan Carr – still the only stoppage loss on the Wiltshire journeyman's record – on a summer evening at Upton Park, mightily impressed those members of Warren's backstage team who had not seen him before.

There were two more one-round triumphs on fleeting visits to Wales, but Evans had to rely

Craig Evans

Evans (left) sizes up a bloody Scott Cardle

on the referees' judgment in his other outings. That proved no problem: he did not lose a round in his first 10 bouts and even when the opposition improved, the Sirhowy Valley product was clearly ahead of the likes of Spaniard Andoni Alonso, Frenchman Dame Seck and combative Scot Ronnie Clark, a future British title challenger. Craig, now part of the Tony Borg academy in Newport, was himself ready for a crack at the Lonsdale Belt.

Four days into a holiday, his father rang to tell him he had been matched with British and Commonwealth super-feather king Liam Walsh at the O2. He trained on the remaining six days of his vacation and then returned home to find that Walsh was fighting Joe Murray instead; Evans had to settle for an eight-rounder against tough, but unambitious Pole Jacek Wylezol on a low-key bill at Wolverhampton – and then damaged his left hand on the way to a points win.

The big chance was not long delayed, however, and he did get to fight at the O2. It came at lightweight, with another unbeaten talent, Scott Cardle, in the opposite corner on May 30, 2015. In retrospect, the opportunity may have been lost at a press conference three days earlier.

Following the obligatory head-to-head for the photographers, Evans extended his hand, Cardle ignored it and Craig angrily flicked the side of the Lancastrian's face. Scott threw himself at the Welshman and security had to pull them apart. The animosity still simmered at the first bell – and it seemed that Evans was the more distracted.

Instead of boxing behind his southpaw jab, Craig was drawn into toe-to-toe exchanges, picking up a nick near the left eye. After being caught, he showed his chin to Cardle and showboated in a needless show of machismo; meanwhile the Scottish-accented Lytham man was collecting the points. Once matters settled in the fifth, Evans showed his skills and kept his rival at bay.

An accidental elbow in the eighth cut Cardle, whose frustration was beginning to show. Yet, with Craig tending to stand off rather than follow up his leads, the Englishman finished strongly to make sure of a unanimous decision, all three judges scoring it 116-112. The margin seemed generous, but Evans's careless concession of the early sessions had left him too much to make up.

He returned five months later against London Olympic team captain Tom Stalker, who had dropped from light-welter and taken on a sports psychologist in an attempt to "bring out his nasty side". The vacant WBO European title was on the line in Manchester on October 10, 2015, Craig going through with it despite the recent death of his grandmother.

Matters were evenly contested early on, but Stalker came on strong in the later rounds, hurting Evans in the last. Londoner Dave Parris had the Welshman in front, but his Belgian colleague gave Stalker a four-point advantage and the German judge could not separate them.

If the consensus regarded Stalker as unfortunate, the reverse was the case when they met again before Christmas and once again found the judges split three ways. This time Craig established his authority early on and even a torrid ninth, in which a head clash cut his right eyebrow and a low blow left him doubled up in agony, seemed insufficient to deny his supremacy. The Hungarian vote went to Evans, but the Italian favoured Stalker, while this time Parris had them level. Once again the WBO European belt was unclaimed.

When they met for the third time, at Cardiff's Motorpoint Arena on November 26, 2016, Stalker was defending the title, having seen off Portuguese Antonio João Bento – just four days short of his 40th birthday – in Liverpool. This time Craig made no mistake.

The Blackwood boxer outworked the visitor in the early rounds, although Tom was never in trouble and landed a few eye-catchers of his own. The only worry for Evans's enthusiastic supporters was the possibility of their man punching himself out, but when he did slow in the sixth there was

Craig beats Tom Stalker at the third attempt and claims the WBO European belt

St Joseph's ABC in Newport – Tony Borg's cradle of champions

no sign of Stalker taking advantage and Craig was able to continue at his own pace until the end. Hungarian judge Ferenc Budai somehow saw them level, but his colleagues agreed that Wales had its first WBO European champion.

Evans faced a tough first defence in Belfast on June 17, 2017, against former holder Stephen Ormond. The clash soon degenerated into something of a wrestling match, with referee Phil Edwards on Craig's case, while allowing the Dubliner to hold with impunity. Eventually the third man seemed to let them get on with it and three times the pair fell, locked together, to the canvas.

Trainer Borg was frustrated at his pupil's failure to box at distance, but he was doing the cleaner work and finished strongly as the 34-year-old Ormond tired. The final half-minute saw Craig deck his man twice and confirm a unanimous victory. The path was open to a possible world title shot.

EDGAR EVANS
(1894-1983)

Welsh Lightweight Champion 1927-28

The farmer's boy from Crumlin could have become a Welsh champion a year earlier than he did. But his innate sportsmanship got in the way.

It was a miracle that Edgar Lewis Evans was there at all. When he was 10 he contracted rheumatic fever and was not expected to survive. But this youngster came from fighting stock and he pulled through to join his four younger brothers in the makeshift gym they set up in a field at Rhiw Farm, training there after a day's strenuous work on the land – and a five-mile run to Penyfan and back.

While Horace, Albert, Reg and Syd all boxed – Albert professionally – Syd made his name as a promoter, becoming the main man in South Wales. But Edgar, who also won competitions in hedging and ditching, was the only one to attain stardom with the gloves on.

His ring promise was evident as an amateur, though there were plenty of losses as Evans travelled far and wide as a pro, swapping punches from Sunderland to Plymouth, Blackpool to London. But his efforts on home ground pushed him into lightweight contention and the 30-year-old was matched with defending champion Billy Moore before a packed house at Crumlin's Palace Theatre on October 12, 1925.

Moore came to the scales nearly half a pound overweight, but Edgar refused to claim a forfeit and the bout went ahead as a title fight. And, although the Penygraig publican dominated early on, the challenger could have claimed victory following an incident in the 17th round when Billy, hurt by a body shot, stumbled through the ropes, ringsiders – and even the referee – helping him return to the stage.

Had Evans protested, the official would have been forced to disqualify Moore, but he shook his head and launched a late assault on the tiring

Edgar Evans

holder in an attempt to earn the belt in what he saw as more honourable fashion. Billy was frequently in trouble, but his tactical nous saw him through to a clear points win.

A month later Moore lost the title – ironically, via disqualification – and Evans set his sights on the new monarch, Billy Ward, from Pentrebach. It took a while, but they came together in Snow's Pavilion, Merthyr, on February 26, 1927. Then, in the second session, a left from Ward drove Edgar to the ropes with such force that the corner-post snapped off at the base, bringing the ropes down with it. The damage proved impossible to repair and the two camps agreed to try again a week later.

Evans's preparation was typical of his career. He spent the day of the bout sowing a field of oats and stepped on the scales to find he was more than two pounds heavy. Somehow, in blizzard conditions, he managed to shed the surplus and played his full part in a thriller, with fluctuating fortunes: Ward was on top early on, with Edgar in trouble in the sixth and seventh, but the Crumlin man recovered to make up the deficit, flooring the tiring champion with a body shot in the 19th. In the last session a left hook knocked Ward out of the ring, and although he made it back in time, another left felled him for the full count.

Edgar's reign lasted 16 months, but only until his first defence. He faced Gordon Cook, like Moore from Penygraig, on July 30, 1928, with the Palace Theatre once again bursting at the seams. The veteran was as game as ever, but too slow to cope with the speedy Rhondda southpaw and C.B. Thomas's decision in the challenger's favour met not a murmur of dissent. It was the last 20-round contest at the weight in Britain.

There were a few sporadic sightings, but, in reality, that was that. But the fighting farmer had been a Welsh champion – and will be remembered as someone who turned down the chance to win the title earlier because it went against his sense of fair play.

JEFF EVANS
(1982-)

🥊 **Welsh Light-Heavyweight Champion 2011-12**

🥊 **Commonwealth Light-Heavyweight Challenger 2011**

The superstitious might say it was an auspicious date. November 11, 2011 – or 11.11.11 – was also, more prosaically, Armistice Day. For Jeff Evans, there was little in the way of either good fortune or peace. But it did put his name in the record books.

The welder and fabricator from Talywain had travelled to Yorkshire to face Jamaican-born Ovill McKenzie for the Commonwealth light-heavyweight belt relinquished by Liverpool's Tony Bellew. But two solid rights, augmented by a thunderous third, sent Evans crashing, his shoulders partly through the ropes at Halifax's North Bridge Leisure Centre. Referee Terry O'Connor called an immediate halt so that paramedics could administer oxygen to the stricken Welshman, who, happily, made a full recovery before leaving the ring.

An official time of just 15 seconds made it the quickest Commonwealth (or Empire) championship fight in history, lasting 10 seconds less than James Hare's light-welter triumph over Namibian Frans Hantindi eight years earlier. But taking on big-punching McKenzie, a previous holder who has since gone on to win the same crown at cruiser and challenge for a world title, was always a big ask. And anyone can be caught cold.

His inadvertent history-making should not detract from the achievements of someone who never laced on a boxing glove until he was 19, when he joined the Pontypool and Panteg club. Even then, he was hardly over-active, with his 20-odd contests including five attempts at the Welsh ABAs with just one appearance in a final, where he was halted by Swansea's Tobias Webb.

Jeff Evans with the Welsh belt

When he decided to turn pro, making his debut three days before his 27th birthday, he chose recently retired Gary Lockett as his mentor, and it proved a wise decision. After three straight points wins, two against Welsh rivals – although awkward Adam Wilcox put him on the deck – 'Jeffro' tried his hand at one of Matchroom's Prizefighter tournaments, widely regarded as a possible short cut to bigger things. But, while he saw off Yorkshireman Peter Federenko, gangling Midlander Paul David, the English super-middle boss, beat him in the semi-final on a split decision.

Moving up to light-heavy, Evans was soon rewarded with a shot at Welsh titleholder Shon Davies, making the first defence of a three-year reign. Fighting in front of his home fans at the Newport Centre on May 7, 2011, the challenger had to withstand an early onslaught from the Welsh-speaker from Gorslas, but the calming words of unflustered mentor Lockett – "For the first time I was listening in the corner," admitted Jeff – helped him take command, bringing blood from the West Walian's nose in the third.

Davies was finding breathing difficult and, after a sixth round in which he was dropped by a left to the ribs, retired on his stool. The belt was heading to the Eastern Valley.

By the end of the year, Evans had had his brief encounter with McKenzie and many expected him to call it a day. But he was determined not to go out on such a note and demonstrated his ability by drawing with unbeaten Lancastrian Matty Clarkson.

Meanwhile, a challenge was heading Jeff's way from someone who had frequently shared his dressing-room at the Newport Centre. Local boy Justyn Hugh, who had won on all eight appearances at the riverside venue, was given his chance there on July 21, 2012, but found Evans distinctly unwilling to let go of the belt. After a tentative start, he was soon controlling matters and leaving the signs of his work on Justyn's face.

Hugh had never travelled beyond six rounds and was expected to fade, but he proved the pundits wrong when he unleashed a series of head shots in the eighth which had Evans, back against the ropes, neither replying nor covering up. Referee Wynford Jones called a halt – and this time Jeff's career was over.

Not his connection with boxing, however. He took charge at his old amateur club and within a year had guided Kieran Gething, son of former pro Gary, to a Welsh elite title.

SELWYN EVANS
(1928-)

🥊 Welsh Lightweight Champion 1951-53

T hey say you should learn from the best. And the Newbridge youngster was able to study at close quarters. When the legendary Joe Louis boxed an exhibition at Newport Athletic Grounds in 1944, Selwyn Evans beat fellow-townsman Harold Urch on the same bill.

With no boxing in the family, Crumlin-born Evans was not originally destined for the ring. In fact, he was taking singing lessons and learning his way around an aria before he laced on a glove. But once he stepped through the ropes it was obvious he had a special talent. A string of age-group successes led to the unique achievement of 1945, when he became the only man to win Welsh junior and senior championships in the same season.

Come 1947 he went all the way to the British ABA feather title and was duly selected for the British team to visit Dublin for the European championships. Some observers thought he had done enough to beat Belgian Jules van Dyk in his first bout, but the judges were not among them.

While other amateur stars jockeyed for places in the following year's London Olympics, Evans opted to turn pro and soon created an impression. When he climbed off the canvas to outpoint Len Davies at Abergavenny it was a result of some significance, given that the Swansea man had just been matched to box for the vacant Welsh feather crown. Davies was beaten by Pontypridd's Jackie Hughes, while Selwyn took a step towards a crack at the new ruler by outscoring Haydn Jones, from Tiryberth, in an official eliminator.

He was back in Abergavenny for the next step but let himself be drawn into a war with a puncher. Dai Davies dropped Evans with a third-round right to the chin and, although things were evenly contested from then on, it was the Skewen man whose arm was raised at the end.

When Selwyn's shot finally came, it was up at lightweight, following the retirement of Reg Quinlan.

Selwyn Evans, then and now

Selwyn's left lead lands on Cliff Anderson, but the Guyanan took the verdict

Opposite him at the Coney Beach Arena on August 22, 1951, was Dennis Sewell, from Nelson, who had outpointed Evans over eight rounds six months earlier. There was to be no repeat.

Sewell was cut along his left eyebrow in the second and Selwyn peppered the injury with jabs until blood was pouring down the side of Dennis's face. The constant barrage had a general weakening effect, as well, and Sewell slumped to the canvas in the eighth. He rose at seven, but at the end of the session the referee decided there was little point in letting things continue. Newbridge had a Welsh titleholder.

Swansea-based manager Eddie Evans took him off to earn a few bob in England – one of many who outpointed him was future British ruler Joe Lucy – but Selwyn fared better when he defended against former victim Len Davies in Carmarthen on March 3, 1952. 'Davo', whose long career included victories over world fly king Jackie Paterson and legend Nel Tarleton, was no longer the speedster of his youth, resorting to holding and spoiling, with the referee repeatedly forced to intervene. By the final bell of a disappointing contest, the champion was well in front.

For his next domestic defence, on November 21, 1952, indoors at the Coney Beach Pavilion, Evans found himself facing another old foe and now his stablemate. Dai Davies was still the national featherweight king, but trying his luck in the higher division. A thrilling contest saw Evans take an early lead, only for Davies to battle back in the later rounds, convincing referee Ike Powell to call it a draw.

The pair tried again on Selwyn's territory, outdoors at Newport's Crindau Park on June 1, 1953, the eve of the Coronation. Davies had to shed a pound and a half in order to make the lightweight limit, but was still the stronger man throughout, decking a lethargic Evans with a head shot in the fourth and two body blows in the ninth. There was little resistance left in the 10th, when Dai claimed two more knockdowns; the first was brief, the second lasted the 10 seconds necessary for the title to change hands.

It proved the final act of the Evans career. Now his ring interests are focussed on his grandsons, while his own physical efforts are devoted to the dance floor; in his late eighties, Selwyn is still strutting his stuff.

JACK FARR
(1915-1995)

🥊 Welsh Light-Heavyweight Champion 1948-49

" There's only one Tommy Farr!" That might have been the chant had pre-war crowds gone in for such things. But in fact there was another valley boxer of that name, although in the ring Thomas John Farr from Abertillery went (mostly) by the name of Jack.

Locally he was known as Tommy, and the lad himself put that on his licence application, but someone else crossed it out and inserted 'Jack' in its place. Given that the 'Tonypandy Terror' was then at the height of his fame, it was a sensible decision.

Collier Farr soon had people talking about him – whatever they called him – with a succession of victories around the Gwent valleys and beyond. But his career slowed to a virtual standstill after he married in 1938, wife

Jack Farr (left) poses with a sparmate

Kit producing a child in each of the next four years; with wartime demands for coal bringing ample overtime, Jack focussed on earning a crust for his expanding family.

Gradually, however, he returned to the ring and although a few losses began to speckle his record, he was mixing with some decent operators, a draw with future Welsh heavyweight challenger Nick Fisher raising a few eyebrows.

Jack was now being mentioned as a contender for the vacant Welsh light-heavyweight title. The authorities took the hint, matching him in an official eliminator against the recently demobbed Billy Phillips, from Senghenydd. But three weeks before the scheduled date Jack came a cropper at the hands of Koffi Kiteman, a useful operator from the Gold Coast, suffering a broken jaw as well as a points defeat. Ironically, as Jack lay in hospital Phillips outpointed Kiteman at Abergavenny. When a collection was taken for the stricken Farr, the African, despite the night's disappointment, donated his entire purse to the fund.

When the damage had healed, the eliminator was rearranged for Abertillery, where a home crowd cheered Jack to a hard-fought points verdict. A fast left lead paved the way for Farr's triumph, with the naturally bigger Phillips's lack of speed telling against him.

The clash for the belt took place over the border at Hereford's Drill Hall on April 28, 1948. Farr was barely above the middleweight limit, conceding nearly a stone to Tiryberth's Elfryn Morris, but it never became an issue, Jack indicating his intentions with a solid right to the jaw to end the first.

Elfryn turned his attentions downstairs over the next few sessions, but Farr's greater technical ability enabled him to take control at distance and he rocked his rival with a right uppercut to open the seventh; failure to realise its effect meant the chance for a stoppage slipped away.

Instead, the Midlands-based Morris – now 31 and a pro since he was 15 – was able to resume his assaults on Farr's stomach and over the following sessions the incessant battering began to take its effect. Jack found a second

A Farr by any other name - 'Tommy' is replaced on his licence application by 'Jack'

wind, however, and his much cleaner punches, still evident as both men tired, earned him C.B. Thomas's decision and the championship belt.

A first-round knockout by middleweight champion Tommy Davies suggested his reign would not be long and, given that Davies then lost to Dennis Powell, few gave Farr much chance when the Mid-Wales man was awarded a title shot at Newtown on July 9, 1949. The fact that Jack was giving away more than 10lb on the scales did little to change that perception.

Farr survived the first solid shot he received and even landed three jabs to the challenger's face. But a few seconds later Powell drove Jack to the ropes and whipped in a left to the body, followed by a short right to the same area and a crunching left to the jaw. Down crashed Farr for the full count. He never boxed again.

Having left the pit to work for the local council, he drove an ashcart in the week and spent Saturdays at the Market Hall, running the market and then acting as MC for the evening's dances. In the rowdy early years of rock'n'roll, his ability with his fists came in handy when there was trouble. And, with no further risk of confusion, everyone once again called him Tommy.

OSSIE HIGGINS
(1931-2000)

🥊 Empire Games Silver Medallist 1958

Winning an Empire Games boxing medal for Wales was never something that featured in the dreams of the young Augustine Robert Higgins. After all, he was a Dubliner – and his ambitions were focussed on the football pitch.

As a teenage centre-forward with Shamrock Rovers he caught the eye of a scout from Aston Villa and moved to Birmingham in 1949. But he never made the first team and was transferred to Ipswich three years later. Despite a hatful of goals for the reserves, he made just two appearances in Division Three (South) – both home defeats – and was released at the end of the season.

By 1957 he was a carpenter's mate, living in Tredegar, and turning out for Abergavenny Thursdays. Looking for some further sporting exercise, Ossie, who had boxed a bit as a junior in his native city, began to frequent a gym near the British Legion Club. His talent was obvious and he soon joined Ebbw Vale ABC.

Victories over Pontypool rugby prop Pedro Diez and Cardiff policeman Alex John earned him the Welsh ABA light-heavy title, a few months

First love - Ossie Higgins in an Ipswich shirt

before Wales hosted the "Friendly Games". He wore the red vest to success against Norway and the Navy, but lost to Coventry boy Johnny Bache in the quarter-finals of the British ABAs – although football was really to blame. Ossie had torn a ligament playing for Ebbw Vale in the Welsh League, but it seemed to have healed; Bache landed a short right to the stomach in the second round and Higgins went down – more in trying to avoid it than from any effect of the punch – and when he went to rise his right leg gave way and the bout was stopped.

There was a further problem when Ossie withdrew from the Wales team to meet the Army, followed by two matches in Belgium, claiming he could no longer make light-heavyweight.

The authorities nevertheless named him for the big one and he saw off Canadian Frank Noneley in an undistinguished quarter-final. (Noneley was lucky to be in Cardiff: he was taking a hiding in a box-off for the team when his opponent swore at the ref and was thrown out.) The fare was so poor that there was a slow handclap after the first two rounds – even with one of their own in the ring, the Welsh fans were losing patience. But in the third, Higgins landed one of the few clean shots thrown, opened a cut near Noneley's eye and the referee called a halt.

Higgins has his arm raised after the Empire Games quarter-final

In the semi-final, Ossie met a Dundee coalman, Willie Bannon, who had floored England's ABA champion Joe Leeming six times en route to a second-round stoppage. The wild-swinging Scot went out to repeat the feat, as Higgins backpedalled frantically to avoid the incoming haymakers. But Ossie began to catch him with good rights on the way in and there were enough of them for his more accurate work overall to clinch the decision.

(Willie may have had to settle for bronze, but he made an impression at the presentation ceremony when he received it from the Duke of Edinburgh. Amateur boxing was a BBC staple in those days and the royal guest was a fan. "I've seen you on TV," said the Duke. "Aye," replied Willie, "and I've seen ye, tae!")

The final saw Higgins well outpointed by Australia's outstanding Tony Madigan. Ossie boxed much better than in previous rounds, but found Madigan particularly durable, soaking up everything the Welshman could get through – and he landed a fair few – and coming back with more.

The Aussie went on to his third Olympics in 1960, reaching the semi-final and losing to a certain Cassius Clay, before retaining his Empire title in Perth. Higgins never boxed again, but remained in Wales until his death in Newport three weeks shy of his 70th birthday.

JUSTYN HUGH
(1984-)

Welsh Light-Heavyweight Champion 2012-14

Boxing is different from all other sports. A football or rugby team with a substantial lead late in the second half is going to win. An athlete 100 yards ahead entering the finishing straight will, barring accidents, breast the tape first. But in the ring, a contest may be heading inexorably in one direction and then, out of the blue, a couple of punches can change everything.

Petshop boy Justyn Hugh – he worked in his Dad's business – proved the point when he took on Welsh light-heavy boss Jeff Evans at the Newport Centre, where both had been regular performers. When they met on July

Justyn Hugh relaxes with his newly acquired belt

21, 2012, Talywain's Evans was rebuilding after a 15-second blast-out by big-hitting Ovill McKenzie in a Commonwealth title bout. At least he had the experience of training to go 12 rounds, unlike Hugh, none of whose bouts had been scheduled for more than 12 minutes. Naturally, the game's prophets saw 'Jeffro' coming on strong in the later stages.

Justyn, originally from the St Julian's area of the city, but living at Rogerstone, was expected to come out fast, which may have accounted for Evans's cautious start. But the holder soon realised that the anticipated pressure was not forthcoming and began to push Hugh back, scoring regularly and controlling the pace. The challenger, his features marking up, was well behind as they entered the second half.

But there was no evidence of any lack of stamina. And, midway through the eighth, Hugh made the points tally irrelevant, unleashing a flurry of blows to the head which sent Evans staggering to the ropes, where he stood as if uncertain how to respond. A little reminiscent of Frank Bruno in similar circumstances, Jeff did not hold on or move, nor did he punch back. Referee Wynford Jones jumped to his rescue and Wales had a new champion.

Justyn came from a sporting family: one great-grandfather, John Stokes, claimed around 500 fights while in the Services, representing both Wales and, while based there, Scotland. Another great-grandfather, Ron Hugh, won international recognition while a midfielder with Newport County.

Their descendant dabbled with boxing as a schoolboy, but began to develop while at Tony Borg's St Joseph's gym. There was little to suggest future stardom, however, with none of his five attempts at the Welsh ABAs reaching a final. But things changed when he turned pro with Chris Sanigar in 2008.

With Borg still calling the shots in training, the popular Hugh became a key ticket-seller on local promotions, collecting nine straight victories to keep everyone happy, before a trip to Sheffield saw him held to a draw by Carl Wild, but a three-round retirement success over North Walian Steffan Hughes primed him for the shot at Evans. Yet the title triumph was his last occasion to celebrate.

In a fragmented career, plagued by shoulder problems, Dean Francis had nevertheless claimed British and European honours at super-middle, followed by British and Commonwealth belts as a light-heavy. After three years out, the Basingstoke man, now a few weeks short of 38, was giving it another go.

Hugh was the chosen foe in a scrap which would see the winner closing in on a Lonsdale Belt. At first it looked as if Justyn would take that step forward as he outjabbed the tentative old-timer for two rounds and dropped him in the third with a right to the temple. Maybe that was a mistake: Francis went up several gears, showing his class in what became a one-sided hammering until referee Jones called a halt in the final session.

After Hugh dropped a close four-rounder to ringwise Nathan King two months later, there was talk of a rematch for the title. But events beyond the ropes meant that would never happen.

In January 2014 the champion appeared at Cardiff Crown Court to admit conspiring to supply drugs, the judge told that he headed a gang who imported £500,000 worth of cocaine. The original 11-year jail sentence was reduced by 12 months on appeal and Hugh was released on licence in 2017.

GEORGE JAMES
(1915-1984)

Welsh Heavyweight Champion 1939-1949

When George James wanted to box, there were no gyms in the Ebbw Vale area. So the kid from Cwm and a few mates – including future flyweight ace Pat Warburton – set up their own. The young miner won a few and decided the ring might offer more rewarding experiences than life at Marine Colliery. So he hit the road with Al Stewart's booth.

As the summer season drew to a close, George left the Gwent valleys for good, moving to London, in traditional fashion, to seek his fortune. But the city promoters' doors stayed firmly shut until the Welsh giant – he was several inches over six feet – was introduced to one of the most colourful characters in the game, Charlie Rose.

London-born Rose had scraped a living in the Australian bush before returning home. He became a columnist on the trade paper, *Boxing,* and eventually added fight manager to his many and varied business roles, looking after the likes of heavyweight champions Phil Scott and Len Harvey. He cast his eyes over the six-foot-plus James, then scaling little more than 12st, and urged him to build himself up and join the big boys.

Victory in a novices' competition at Wembley in 1937 provided substance to back Rose's one-man publicity machine, but it was at home – or, at least, in Mountain Ash – that he was given the chance to succeed Tommy Farr on the Welsh heavyweight throne. More than 10,000 packed the Pavilion on February 21, 1938, to see him take on Jim Wilde, and, despite giving away more than a stone, dominate the Swansea man, whose left eye, first damaged in the second, was almost closed by the fourth.

George James

Big Jim lacked nothing when it came to heart, however, and he battled on one-eyed through the middle rounds and even came close to halting James in a torrid 10th. That was pretty much Wilde's last hurrah, though; as he tired, his blows strayed below the waist and the referee had warned him three times before finally disqualifying him with barely a minute of the 15 rounds remaining.

Stablemate Harvey described George as "the best prospect I have encountered for many

James does his exercises with trainer Harry Goodman, watched by stablemate Tommy Farr

years" and claimed that he already had a better knowledge of the scientific side of boxing than countryman Farr. It was not the only praise coming his way. After James knocked out Frank Hough at Somerton Park, the Londoner took the mic to pronounce that his conqueror "would go on to win greater honours". It was a sporting gesture and well received, but proved optimistic.

Despite his new popularity in the Smoke, where he now lived, George was still an attraction back home and Cardiff's Greyfriars Hall was rammed to watch him defy a septic toe and knock out former British titleholder Ben Foord. That proved something of a false dawn.

Ex-Empire champion Larry Gains, celebrating his 37th birthday, outpointed James, as did future British ruler Jack London, but George was still good enough to defend his belt in a rematch with Wilde on the challenger's territory at the Mannesmann Hall on July 24, 1939. James – with national hero Farr in his corner – dropped Jim in the fifth and repeated the feat six rounds later, by which time Wilde was in a bad way. Midway through the 11th, he indicated that he could not see and his cornermen threw in the towel.

With the outbreak of World War I, George enlisted in the RAF as a PTI and boxed little beyond the odd exhibition during his spell in uniform. When he was demobbed in 1945, he linked up with Wally May, a Cockney, but a protégé of the renowned Swansea-born trainer, Dai Dollings. May liked what he saw in the gym and optimistically forecast that his new charge would make even recently crowned British and Empire boss Bruce Woodcock sit up and take notice.

It turned out differently: Woodcock floored him five times for a third-round defeat in non-title action. And there were three more stoppage losses, the last seeing the loss of his Welsh crown and the end of his career.

Dennis Powell, Monmouthshire-born, but based in Mid Wales, had just claimed the Welsh title at light-heavy and would go on to become British champion at that weight. Across the border in Oswestry on August 6, 1949, Powell stormed after George from the first bell. The Cwm fighter looked rusty and slow, two left hooks leaving him draped over the ropes at the end of the opener. Early in the second James was felled by a right cross and a follow-up attack climaxed with a vicious left hook which left the 33-year-old unable to beat the count.

Having fallen in love with Bournemouth when posted there during the war, he settled in the Dorset resort, working as a carpenter for a large building firm. It was while on a job in Bristol that he was rushed to hospital with a blocked artery in his left leg. But complications set in and he was critically ill for a week, eventually having the limb amputated.

James lived on to the age of 68 and is commemorated in his adopted home by a plaque on a park bench.

HAYDN JONES
(1927-2010)

Welsh Featherweight Champion 1953

When the Welsh ABA championships resumed after World War II, the boys from Tiryberth ABC were ready. With former pro Glyn Agland at the helm, the Rhymney Valley club had three finalists, two of them victorious. Lightweight Eddie Lewis, who beat a young Eddie Thomas en route, never turned pro. But flyweight Haydn Jones was to rule Wales in that sphere as well.

One of those disputes that always seem to disrupt amateur boxing prompted the 19-year-old to make the switch. Described as an exponent of the "Jim Driscoll style of boxing", Haydn settled quickly, with eight victories on the trot after a points loss in his debut, when he was ambitiously matched against Nantyglo's Billy Davies, winner of the Welsh flyweight title just six months later.

But championship aspirations were consigned to the back burner when he lost five in a row. Future Welsh bantam boss Jackie Sutton outpointed him and, after a year out, his London bow saw him flattened by Mickey Forrester. Less than two weeks later – no mandatory suspensions then – he ran Newbridge rival Selwyn Evans so close that their rematch three months later was recognised as a Welsh feather eliminator; the result was the same. When Rhondda-born Midlander Tommy Jones knocked him out in three, Haydn walked away from the ring.

Three years later he was back, overcoming a first-round knockdown to draw with that man Evans, who had become Welsh lightweight king in the interim. When long-serving Welsh feather champion Dai Davies announced his retirement, leaving mandatory challenger Dave Lloyd without an opponent, Jones was called up to contest the vacant title at Sophia Gardens Pavilion on February 16, 1953. The Swansea man's greater experience enabled him to control the early

Haydn Jones

rounds, but bit by bit Haydn's body blows worked on the 30-year-old's stamina.

Lloyd was flagging throughout the later stages and survival was his only real ambition. This he managed, but he was unable to prevent the stand-in opponent taking the crown. Not that Dave agreed with referee Ike Powell.

He demanded a return, waving £25 in crisp notes to demonstrate the seriousness of his intentions. And Haydn, hampered first time around by the effects of flu, was happy to oblige, the pair coming together for a second time at the Pier Pavilion in Rhyl on May 4, 1953.

Indeed, it was Lloyd who looked apprehensive, trying to claim his man inside in a bid to avoid a repetition of the assault downstairs he remembered too well from Cardiff. The manoeuvre had limited success, red blotches on Dave's torso demonstrating how much had still got through, although when Haydn switched to the head, he was lectured for failure to close the glove. A left to the mouth stopped Jones in his tracks in the sixth, but he coasted the later rounds to claim a comfortable decision.

Welsh bantam champion Hughie Thomas, younger brother of British welter ruler Eddie, was eyeing the possibility of a second title and the Welsh Area Council agreed that he should meet Jones at 9st 2lb, saying that if Thomas put up a decent show they would approve him as a featherweight challenger. He did more than that: after a slow start, the Merthyr man took over and, despite a late revival by Haydn, held on to take the decision.

Three months later, on October 26, 1953, the pair were back at Sophia Gardens to contest the belt. Not that the fare they served up really merited championship status, *Boxing News* dismissing it as "one of the dreariest contests ever witnessed" at the Cardiff venue. Referee Bill Bevan was already calling for more action in the first, but apart from the odd left lead from Thomas and an occasional two-handed body assault by Jones there was little response.

Bevan managed to find a winner after 12 rounds and it was Haydn who kept his crown. Whether he was so disillusioned by his own performance or stung by the criticism, he never laced up the gloves again.

J.D. JONES
(1905-1992)

Empire Games Silver Medallist 1934

They called him 'Dinky Doo' in the Royal Welch Fusiliers. But John David Jones was a man who had earned the respect of his fellow soldiers, no matter how naff his nickname. After all, even the most truculent squaddie was unlikely to take advantage of an NCO who had won four Army boxing championships.

One of nine children – and none of his six brothers ever laced up the gloves – the boy from Senghenydd followed his father down the pit when he left school. But life underground was not to his taste and in 1925 he joined up and soon found his way to the gym, where his natural ability saw him win a novices' competition.

The titles then came thick and fast. Battalion honours, then the Rhine Army while he served in Germany, followed by a quartet of full Army successes. Three years running Jones went on to conquer the best the Navy and Air Force could provide in the Imperial Services tournament. In 1933, however, he lost to an airman and later that year announced that he was retiring from all representative action, confining himself to the regimental team.

Fortunately, he was persuaded to change his mind and enter the trials for the Wales party to attend the 1934 Empire Games. In a box-off at Cardiff's St Patrick's Hall, Johnny met the Welsh ABA featherweight champion, city boy Ron Brabyn, outpointing him on the referee's casting vote.

But his preparation for the big event at Wembley was hampered when he suffered an eye injury in the very last minute of his training. Despite the handicap he was able to hold off the rushes of Canadian Sam Tomlinson in "really workmanlike style" and reach the final.

J.D. Jones

There the Aber Valley product met South African Charles Catterall, eight years younger than the "hero of 100 fights", as J.D. was described. Catterall's greater speed and agility saw him home to a victory cheered to the echo by his country's athletes and swimmers in the crowd.

The Springbok went on to reach the final of the Berlin Olympics two years later, but Jones's ring career was winding down – though he was one of only two Welsh winners in a 5-2 defeat by Ireland at the Welsh White City in Cardiff, where the boxing was followed by an evening's greyhound racing to raise cash for Jim Driscoll's favourite charity, the Nazareth House orphanage.

Johnny spent much of World War II in Burma, fighting in the Arakan campaign, and was mentioned in dispatches on three occasions. When he was demobbed in 1948, after 21 years, he settled in his wife's home town, Redhill, Surrey, and began a 25-year stint with the Post Office.

On his retirement they moved to Scotland to live near their daughter and it was at Inverurie, near Aberdeen, that Johnny, by now a white-bearded patriarch, died at the age of 86. And, despite those famous initials, it turned out his name was David John all the time!

KEITH JONES
(1968-)

🥊 Welsh Welterweight Champion 2002-03

Every underdog has his day, as the proverb nearly says. For the stocky southpaw from Cefn Hengoed, that came on September 15, 2002, when he faced hometown hero Ross McCord on a Sunday afternoon at Swansea Leisure Centre for the vacant Welsh welterweight throne. It was the 78th fight of Keith Jones's career; he had won only seven and the last of those victories was more than two years earlier.

Ross's father, Frank, having failed in three Welsh title bids of his own, was ready to shell out for a belt for his boy, with the cash-strapped area council unable to provide one. Few doubted his confidence was well placed.

But that overlooked one significant factor. This was not the usual short-notice job for the shaven-headed Jones, happy to go through the motions against a local ticket-seller. This time Keith had a national championship in his sights and time to prepare.

McCord had never been beyond six rounds and was wary of running out of steam. He need not have worried. Jones attacked from the first bell, ignoring Ross's left leads to go to the body with the sort of artillery few realised he might have in his locker. The second session saw McCord forced to the ropes and the third opened with him on the canvas, although referee Roddy Evans ticked Keith off for straying below the line. When Ross was dropped again, however, the blow was legal, but the gong postponed the finale into the fourth, when a series of right uppercuts floored the Swansea man once more and this time it was all over.

There was a stunned silence before the crowd joined the sporting McCord clan in applauding the ecstatic new titleholder. But there was one more reminder that this outcome had not been intended: to keep the belt with which he had been

Keith Jones

presented, Jones had to dig into his purse money for £100, the sum his victim's dad had agreed to pay.

The surprise new champion had, in fact, seen title action before in a pro career that began eight years earlier, though he lost two years to asthma picked up by inhaling paint fumes at his factory job. When he returned to the ring he actually went on a five-fight unbeaten run before normal service was resumed.

But after acquiring one of the low-rent British Masters titles with a cut-eye stoppage of Mark McGowan in Plymouth, Keith was accepted as a challenger to Welsh light-welter ruler Jason Cook at Swansea Leisure Centre on May 12, 2000. Jones, who took a day off work for the occasion, began behind a high guard, hoping former amateur star Cook would fade. But allowing the Maesteg man to set his own pace more or less guaranteed that would not happen and referee Mike Heatherwick gave his fellow-townsman every round.

Keith claimed an injury win next time out, but added just one draw in his next 30 contests prior to that shock against McCord. Coincidentally, a Welsh championship tussle was again followed by a cut-eye triumph – but that was the last time he left the ring victorious.

The crown was lost to Swansea stylist Jason Williams at Aberystwyth Arts Centre on February 23, 2003, when Keith's dominance in the middle rounds – the trademark grunts which went with his power shots were noisy evidence of his success – was not enough to outweigh Williams's control in the early and late sessions.

Jones had one more tilt at glory, celebrating his 100th bout by tackling former British title challenger Bradley Pryce at the Newport Centre on July 3, 2004, with his old welter belt on the line. Keith did himself proud, but the lanky Pryce eventually forced an eighth-round finish. Keith was consoled with an engraved cup to mark his centenary.

After seven more outings, Jones, nearing 37, finally hung up those busy gloves. In all, he faced no fewer than 25 boxers who won British titles or better and another 11 who challenged for those honours. Not bad for a so-called journeyman.

TREVOR LLEWELLYN
(1897-1981)

Welsh Heavyweight Champion 1922-23

Abig-punching heavyweight always causes a stir. And when PC Trevor Llewellyn captured the Welsh amateur title inside a round, people took notice.

Maybe not his father, a 5ft 7in docker who had somehow produced a 6ft 3in son. He rarely even made the effort to watch his offspring in action. But others beyond the Pill area of Newport were quick to see the financial possibilities.

Perhaps they were too ambitious. The youngster was already 23 and keen to make the big time, happily heading for London and the sort of novice tournament that could provide a short cut to stardom. Not for Trevor.

Yet it was another defeat, on a charity card at the Stow Hill Drill Hall, which demonstrated genuine promise. Gipsy Daniels, although still five years from capturing the British light-heavy crown, had already picked up a wealth of experience before he faced Llewellyn, yet many had the local ahead after 10 rounds. The last five saw the Llanelli man come on strong to take a deserved verdict, but the loser had shown he had a lot going for him.

Another London tournament ended in failure, so he focussed on his own patch. At Lime Street Drill Hall, he knocked out Jack Tyrrell and the Lyceum Theatre saw him outpoint Bob Allison, victories all the more popular as they came against Cardiff rugby players!

Llewellyn was rewarded with a shot at the vacant Welsh throne. On August 19,

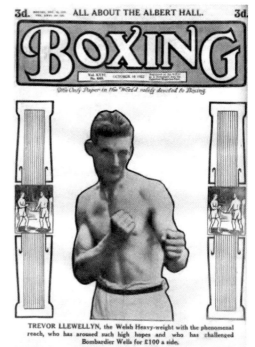

TREVOR LLEWELLYN, the Welsh Heavy-weight with the phenomenal reach, who has aroused such high hopes and who has challenged Bombardier Wells for £100 a side.

Trevor Llewellyn makes the big time on the cover of Boxing

Trevor (fourth from left, at back) with the Newport Docks rugby team in 1920-21. Third from the right in the front row is fellow boxer Jerry Shea, who actually played for Wales that season, yet still turned out for his works side!

1922, just 18 months after he had claimed the amateur title at Newport Athletic Club, he again had home advantage when he faced Tom Norris at the Empire Music Hall in Charles Street.

Norris, one of four boxing brothers from Clydach Vale, started the faster, drawing blood from Trevor's nose, but when Tom stormed in to finish the affair, Llewellyn whipped over a fast counter and Tom slumped to the floor for five seconds. The Rhondda man was driven back to his corner under severe fire, but his defence was good enough to see him to the bell.

In the second Tom walked on to another counter and suffered another visit to the boards, but when Llewellyn forced him to the ropes, a bolt snapped and one of the strands came loose, giving Norris a welcome break while the problem was fixed.

In the third, Trevor stopped waiting and instigated the action. Three uppercuts sent his opponent down for three counts and Norris was being overwhelmed by the tide of blows when referee Charlie Barnett jumped in to call a halt.

Feeling he was ready to aim at the top, his backers brought in Guardsman Charlie Penwill to face the new prodigy at the Drill Hall in Cardiff six weeks later. In the event, the gamble half-worked. For 20 rounds in front of a huge crowd, Llewellyn proved he was worthy of his recent hype. Then referee Jack Smith gave the verdict to Penwill and the crowd went bananas. Mr Barnett, this time in the role of matchmaker, conceded Charlie probably deserved the nod, but he was thrilled with Llewellyn's performance, as was his ringside neighbour, top London promoter Major Arnold Wilson. .

Team Llewellyn were invited to the Albert Hall to challenge Bombardier Billy Wells, but the former champion, now 33, was starched by Jack Bloomfield and that plan went by the board. Instead, Australian Albert Lloyd was hired to visit Cardiff and put the policeman to the test. It proved disastrous. Although Trevor kept fighting back, he was pulled out during the 19th round. And there was another stoppage loss before he defended his Welsh crown against former victim Allison on February 5, 1923, at the Stow Hill venue where he had faced Daniels. But the champion – although a teetotaller and non-smoker, the latter as rare in those days as the former – did not train with any enthusiasm.

The first five rounds saw Llewellyn forcing the pace, but shipping occasional solid shots as he did so. Come the sixth, the local hero was flagging. The following session saw him forced through the ropes and on to his back; he resumed the fight, but shortly afterwards the towel floated in.

By 1926 Trevor had seemingly given up on even a token training regime, something that was underlined when he faced ex-copper Frank Stephens, a former Cardiff rugby star who had gone north. Llewellyn outboxed the Pontlottyn man in the first, but had blown a gasket by the second and gave up at the end of the session.

There were further defeats in London and Manchester as well as Wales, with old foe Tom Norris among his conquerors, and a clear-cut points loss against Crumlin newcomer Dick Power – later to follow Llewellyn to the Welsh title – across the border at Lydney.

Trevor's ring career was on its last legs, but he kept pounding his beat at Newport Docks until leaving the force in 1963, eventually reaching the good old age of 83.

GARY LOCKETT
(1976-)

- WBC and WBO Middleweight Challenger 2008

- WBU Middleweight Champion 2006-08

- WBO Inter-Continental Light-Middleweight Champion 2002

- European U-16 Gold Medallist 1992

When one of Wales's hardest-hitting amateurs turned pro, expectations were high. Yet Gary Lockett's career almost suffered a knockout blow from a creature so small it could not be seen by the naked eye. Just a few weeks into life in the paid ranks, all seemed over.

The Cwmbran puncher had been feeling exhausted after a couple of minutes' exercise and nobody knew why. It took doctors a year to come up with the answer: Gary was allergic to a certain type of mite in house dust. The cure was simple. A cover over his mattress was enough. But there was another year of shelf-stacking at KwikSave before the Board of Control, who had suspended him in the belief that he was asthmatic, were sufficiently convinced to restore his licence.

Gary Lockett

The decision was a huge relief, not merely to the lad himself, but to those hardcore fight fans who had watched with enthusiastic anticipation as he cut a swathe through the junior ranks. The son of a builder and a school cook, young Lockett showed sporting talent on the rugby field, representing Gwent Under-14s at full-back in a line-up including future Wales star Ian Gough, but frequent injuries prompted him to give up and focus on the ring, where he was already making waves.

Having won his first bout in 12 seconds, he nevertheless lost five of his 11 bouts while with the local Coed Eva club, but a switch to Pontypool and Panteg brought him under the influence of top coach Tony Williams and the trophies began to mount up.

There were five Welsh schoolboy titles, four in the boys' clubs tournament and two more at youth; four times he converted them into British honours, as well as three times winning the *Daily Star* Golden Gloves competition, with the first success, in Cardiff, seeing the 14-year-old introduced to the Welsh public via a confident interview with legendary commentator Hugh Johns.

A young Gary wears his Welsh vest with pride

The peak of his amateur success came two years later when he struck gold in the inaugural European Under-16 championships in Italy, stopping all three rivals. His one shot at the senior Welsh ABAs, however, ended in anti-climax with defeat in the prelims by RAF man Sean Pepperall. The teenager promptly turned pro with former Olympian John Hyland, then promoting regularly on Merseyside.

Gary's first 16 contests – with that enforced two-year gap – brought 16 wins, only three foes lasting the course, as trainer Colin Moorcroft smoothed the rough edges. Hyland and Liverpool-based Irishman Brendan Devine made way for a promotional flirtation with Barry Hearn before Lockett signed with Frank Warren and collected the WBO Inter-Continental light-middle belt on a Ricky Hatton bill in Manchester on February 9, 2002, knocking out former WBA title challenger Kevin Kelly in the fourth to hand the Aussie his first stoppage loss.

But Kelly had demonstrated defensive weaknesses in the Welshman and they were to prove disastrous when he risked his new crown against stocky Russian Yuri Tsarenko in front of US cameras, at Cardiff International Arena for the Joe Calzaghe-Charles Brewer showdown. Damage to both hands restricted Gary's attacking ambitions, but his lack of head movement was mainly responsible for a broken nose and fractured cheekbone as he went down to a split-decision defeat.

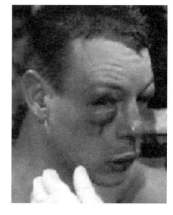

It was seven months before Lockett returned, at middleweight, with veteran Brian Hughes in charge, and he duly took all eight rounds against Ukrainian tough guy Victor Fesechko. Revenge over Tsarenko followed, before another bump on the rocky road to the top.

Michael Monaghan, a Nottingham-Irishman who had been in Wales to spar with Calzaghe, was the

Battered and beaten - Lockett after the first Tsarenko fight

opponent at the CIA and had significant support from the home crowd in his anguish at seeing Gary's arm raised after 10 rounds. The winner was equally dissatisfied after a flat performance and complained of a migraine before heading for hospital to be checked out.

After an eight-month break – and surgery on his nose – Lockett was back, halting four successive foes, including Monaghan in a rematch in Newport, before a visit to Rome and a points victory over useful Beninois Victor Kpadenou. Warren rewarded him with a shot at the vacant WBU middle title on home soil at the Newport Centre on March 11, 2006.

In the opposite corner, replacing the injured Ryan Rhodes, was Guyana-born Gilbert Eastman, brother of world title challenger Howard and himself Southern Area champion, but at light-middle. *Boxing News* had labelled the pair "the oldest prospects in town", with neither Gary, at 29, nor his 33-year-old rival having fulfilled their initial promise. Eastman never would. One solid right ended matters inside a round, sending the Londoner into a four-fight losing streak and enforced retirement.

The Rhodes fight was rearranged for the Millennium Stadium in July, with Lockett preparing in Thailand with Swansea-based conditioning coach Paul Wheel, although the finishing touches were added by Hughes in Manchester. Ryan had left the Ingle camp after 20 years – though he was still only 29 – and linked up with ex-stablemate Dave Coldwell; he showed the silkier skills, but was let down by his workrate.

When Gary put the switch-hitting Sheffielder on the deck with a left hook in the opener, an early night seemed likely, but Rhodes recovered to have the home fighter badly marked up before dropping him in the 10th, the first count of Lockett's career. He was unable to finish matters, however, and the Welshman took a clear unanimous verdict.

He was back at the iconic stadium for his next defence nine months later, but the corner had a different look. The birth of son Jac meant Gary no longer wanted to spend so much time away from his Pontyclun home, so

he joined the thriving Enzo Calzaghe gym at Cwmcarn. Wigan southpaw Lee Blundell – tall and slim, with dyed-blond hair and pale skin, he resembled a stick of celery – could boast a stoppage win over Rhodes, but never troubled Lockett, who felled him

Lockett moves in on Ryan Rhodes

three times en route to a third-round finish.

Gary, who has never regarded the WBU belt as a "proper" world championship, was offered a shot at the IBF king, Arthur Abraham, but rejected it because it paid only £30,000 and would have given the German promoters the right to stage his next five fights if he won. Always a realist where the money-or-glory equation was concerned, Lockett was far more receptive when a cheque four times the size was

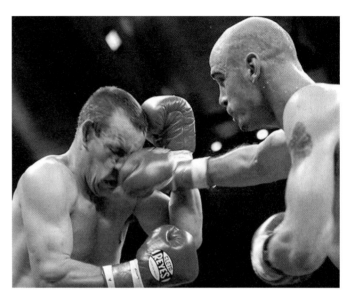

End of the road - Gary under fire from Kelly Pavlik

waved in his direction as reward for tackling man-of-the-moment Kelly Pavlik for his WBC and WBO belts in Atlantic City on June 7, 2008.

The 26-year-old Youngstown man was the talk of the fight game. Not only did he, unlike most US fighters, take thousands of fans from Ohio to watch him in action, but those travelling supporters had seen 33 straight victories, culminating in two thrillers against long-time champion Jermain Taylor. Pavlik was later to decline into alcoholism, but when he met Lockett he was at his peak. The bookies had the American at 16-1 on, with 9-1 against a Welsh victory. Gary agreed with them. "My only chance was to land a big punch before he did," he says.

It never happened. Back at the Boardwalk Hall, scene of his come-from-behind title-winning triumph nine months earlier, Pavlik brought blood from Lockett's nose in the first. The challenger had sparred with Enzo Maccarinelli in preparation, but still found Kelly too tall and too big; rarely able to land a clean shot, he instead shipped regular punishment and took a knee in the second. A more involuntary knockdown followed before the bell came to his aid.

A desperate Lockett assault to open the third had little impact on the champion, who responded with a right to the temple which sent Gary reeling across the ring. He rose at nine, but referee Eddie Cotton had seen enough – and there were no arguments from the Welsh camp.

Trainer Gary celebrates victory with British champion Liam Williams

Lockett, his bank balance duly enhanced, walked away from the sport to focus on his property interests. But he could not stay away, becoming a manager and trainer and soon making his name outside the ropes. He steered Rhondda boy Liam Williams to British and Commonwealth titles and was in the corner when West Countryman Nick Blackwell claimed an unexpected Lonsdale Belt. He was also there when Blackwell collapsed after fighting Chris Eubank, Jr, taking unwarranted stick from fistically illiterate observers for his perceived failure to intervene.

Tragically, lightning was to strike twice, with Gary forced to watch helplessly from the opposite corner when Scot Mike Towell was fatally injured in a British title eliminator with West Walian Dale Evans.

The two events prompted much soul-searching by a man who had always claimed not to like boxing that much. But, happily, Gary Lockett decided to persevere and he seems destined to be around the gyms for a long time to come.

BEN MARSHALL
(c1904-????)

Welsh Welterweight Champion 1927-30

In an era when most working-class men punched for pay from an early age and many amateurs scorned the pro game, gipsy Ben Marshall flourished in both. Trained as an amateur at Newport Central by Tom Stradling, himself a former Welsh ABA champion but better known as a wrestler, he won Welsh and British titles, and reached a semi-final at the 1925 Europeans, losing a box-off for the bronze medal.

But after eight months out of work, he had to forget dreams of the 1928 Olympics and start turning his skills into hard cash. His pedigree meant Marshall was thrust straight into title contention. His debut brought victory over Taffs Well's Billy Green, a man who had already challenged for the Welsh welter crown, while his next outing, against Roy Martin, was billed as an eliminator for that honour. The Crumlin man was despatched in seven rounds.

Next up was former champion Billy Moore, outpointed after stepping in at the last minute when original foe Tommy Morgan's mother died hours before the show. And just one week later, on March

Ben Marshall

21, 1927, Marshall was back at the Stow Hill Pavilion to dethrone Welsh welter champion Tom Thomas in only his fourth professional fight, collecting an ornate gold belt put up by promoter Jake Channing.

The challenger came in a pound and a quarter overweight, but was able to shed it in the allotted hour. Any doubts over his stamina were never tested. In the second, Ben moved in behind repeat jabs and rocked Thomas with a right, before a follow-up flurry dropped him for five. The Deri fighter showed a degree of desperation in the next few rounds, with Marshall's straighter shots picking up points until he decked Tom again in the sixth, the punch also opening a cut beneath his right eye. The injury troubled him in a toe-to-toe seventh, when he was floored twice, but survived to the bell only for his cornermen to shy in the towel.

Ben's first defence came four months later in Pontypridd against Billy Ward, from Pentrebach. The choice brought protests from Moore, but Marshall had insisted on a substantial sidestake and, unlike the former ruler, Ward came up with the money. His backers must have regretted their enthusiasm as it proved one of the traveller's easiest nights: he staggered Billy with a big right in the opening seconds and the recipient seemed to lose heart. He was rocked in the sixth and although he managed to stay on his feet until the bell, his seconds pulled him out.

Moore had his chance before the year ended, though only in a 10-round non-title exercise, and proceeded to floor Marshall before having to retire with a damaged thumb. Once the Rhondda veteran recovered, the pair tried again – and this time it ended in a draw. Oldham middleweight Joe Higginbotham also finished level with Ben at Liverpool Stadium, but they were the only blemishes on his record in Britain.

It had been more than a year since the Newportonian had risked his title, but it was on the line when he met Billy Thomas, brother of the man he had dethroned, in Bridgend on October 6, 1928. Marshall kept his crown – and his unbeaten record – but it was controversial. Thomas's brilliant defence frustrated the holder early on, while his counters seemed to give him a solid lead. Ben battled back and a couple of solid hooks in the 10th had his rival hanging on while his head cleared; without apparent warning, referee Billy Morgan wrenched the two apart and promptly disqualified the challenger.

The following year Marshall followed a well-worn trail and sailed for Australia, where the money was good and British visitors were popular. But his invincibility was shattered on his first appearance, against national champion Jack Carroll at the Sydney Stadium. Ben's right eye was gashed and closed in the sixth; after 10 rounds the damage was so bad that the referee called a halt.

Ben responded with a decision over American Jimmy Mollette, but was then knocked out in two by Jack Haines before heading for home. Haines was half a stone heavier, but the result will have been a shock to Marshall, who was so proud of his sturdy jaw that once, at a fair, he had thrilled the crowd by getting them to balance a huge steel-rimmed wagon wheel on his chin.

While Ben was Down Under, Billy Fry began to call himself the "residential" Welsh welter champion and the Board ordered the real monarch to defend against him. But the purse he was offered did not meet Marshall's expectations, which had been inflated by the generous sums he earned in Australia. The authority had little sympathy and stripped him of his crown.

At least Ben's financial desires were met at Royton when he took on Lancastrian Joe Rostron, a recent conqueror of the great Jock McAvoy, in one of the biggest money matches ever seen in the North of England. The Welshman's pleasure will have been enhanced by a points win, but it marked the last act of his ring career.

Though he never fought again, Ben was still fit well into old age and fond of demonstrating his party trick: he could walk on his hands for a quarter of a mile!

KEVIN McCORMACK
(1967-)

🏅 European Bronze Medallist 1993

One of Wales's greatest amateur boxers only took up the sport to avoid having to go to bed early. Seven-year-old Kevin McCormack's parents were pretty strict about when he and brother Brendan were to be home at night, but they found a way around the curfew. In the same Cwmbran street lived the Manley family, whose kids attended Coed Eva ABC, run by big brothers Mike and Chris, and the McCormack boys, realising that meant staying out a while longer, asked to join them.

"When we got there, we loved it," recalls Kevin. That enthusiasm was accompanied by sufficient ability to see him win a record 11 Welsh ABA titles.

Coached from the start by Chris Manley, he picked up four Welsh schools titles and another at youth level, before claiming his first senior honour as a teenage heavyweight and repeating the feat the following year. But progress at British level stalled in the ABA semi-finals, once against future WBO champion Henry Akinwande, and Kevin thought of retirement.

Manley talked him out of it, suggesting a move up to the recently created super-heavy class. McCormack, at 6ft 4in – both his parents were six-footers – had struggled with the scales and the new division put an end to that. The move, in 1988, was immediately rewarded with a British title to go with the Welsh. Not before a bizarre semi-final victory, however: floored three times by Midlander Clifton Mitchell, Kevin looked certain to lose the verdict, but a judge pointed out to the referee that Mitchell had bitten the Welshman on the neck in the third round. When another judge confirmed this, the guilty man was belatedly disqualified and McCormack went through to the final and a unanimous decision over Lydney's bigger Steve Woollaston.

Kevin McCormack

He went on to claim two more British titles, the only non-Londoner to win the super-heavy crown in the first nine years of its existence. Naturally, there was interest from the pro side: after a sparring session with Lennox Lewis, the future world champion's manager, Frank Maloney, made him an offer. But Kevin's father advised him to focus on a more secure career and he opted to join the Royal Marines.

Kevin won three Combined Services championships, but remained loyal to Wales, marching on to his title record, while representing his country all over the world. Three times he competed at Commonwealth Games, twice losing to the eventual gold medallist, but it was a European event in Turkey which saw him make the podium.

McCormack began with a comfortable 6-2 victory over southpaw Slavisa Jankovic, a Yugoslav boxing as an independent while civil war raged in his homeland, and his quarter-final was over inside a round. Ukrainian Oleg Belikov had eye damage from his previous bout and after some even exchanges the Romanian referee called up the ringside doctor to check it out. The medic ruled Oleg could not continue and Wales was guaranteed a medal.

McCormack had to settle for bronze, however, his workrate never matching that of barrel-chested Bulgarian Svilen Rusinov, who forced the pace throughout – even if the computer scoring gave him a strange-looking 3-0 victory. At least Kevin could console himself that he lost to the best – Rusinov edged out a Georgian in the final.

The Marine had another crack at the continental championship three years later in Denmark, where a quarter-final spot would ensure a trip to the summer's Atlanta Olympics. But luck deserted McCormack: first he drew top seed Alexei Lezin, a Russian southpaw, and then suffered a cut right eye which saw the

Flag bearer - Kevin leads the way for the Wales Commonwealth Games team

doctor call a halt in the third. Lezin went on to take gold with a decision over a certain Wladimir Klitschko.

The Welsh titles kept coming, but events in 1998 left Kevin disillusioned. A kidney infection prevented him adding a 12th national honour and the selectors chose the new champion, Mark Flynn, to go to the Commonwealth Games in Kuala Lumpur. A fit-again Kevin, desperate for a record fourth trip, persuaded the authorities to pick him against Scotland, duly halting that country's Games choice, and then to allow him a box-off with Flynn. Despite appearing to dominate, Kevin was adjudged to have lost on countback – and that was that.

When he left the Marines 19 years ago, McCormack turned his attention to football, becoming kitman at Portsmouth, a post he still holds. The high point – if a little bittersweet for a Welshman – came when he was the man responsible for making sure all the gear was safely transported to Wembley for their 2008 FA Cup victory over Cardiff City.

As for boxing, he actually made a comeback a couple of years ago, training for 14 weeks before taking part in a charity bout which raised £50,000 towards caravans to provide holidays for sick children.

SEAN McGOLDRICK
(1991-)

🥊 **Commonwealth Games Gold Medallist 2010**

🥊 **Commonwealth Games Bronze Medallist 2014**

Eight months after the closing ceremony of the 2010 Commonwealth Games in India, the last gold medal was placed around the neck of Welshman Sean McGoldrick.

Then just 18 and studying for his A-levels, the Newport bantamweight had lost the final to Sri Lankan Manju Wanniarachchi and was duly awarded silver. But the winner failed a drugs test and, although it took an age to exhaust the various appeal processes, in due course McGoldrick was confirmed as the champion.

In a ceremony at Cardiff's Welsh Institute of Sport, he was finally presented with his prize by Mike Hooper, Chief Executive Officer of the Commonwealth Games Federation. It marked the high point of a journey which began when the 10-year-old from Duffryn first climbed the steps of St Joseph's ABC.

Big brother Liam was already training there, while younger sibling Tom followed, but neither had the dedication of Sean, who picked up two Welsh youth titles and a British boys' clubs trophy in a stellar junior career.

His first year as a senior brought him the Welsh ABA bantam championship, clinched with a points win over former junior conqueror – and future Olympian – Joe Cordina. And come October he was selected in a nine–man team for New Delhi.

McGoldrick comfortably outscored Ghanaian Jessie Lartey, then edged out Ulsterman Tyrone McCullagh and ringwise Mauritian Bruno Julie, each by a single point, to face 30-year-old Wanniarachchi in a final involving two men with similar styles, each punching in bursts from behind tight defences. It was on a knife edge throughout, with no more than a point between them at any stage; the last scoring shot

Sean McGoldrick with his Commonwealth silver ...

... which is replaced in due course by the gold

came from the Welshman to leave the pair level at 7-7 at the final bell, only for the Sri Lankan to get the nod on countback.

But the veteran's urine sample showed traces of nandrolone. Manju claimed he had taken it unwittingly in medication for asthma, but his pleas were rejected and he promptly retired from the sport. For the newly instated champion, it was only the start.

Sean snubbed offers to go pro and kept busy on the international scene. But while he picked up further Welsh titles on the only two occasions he entered, glory at a higher level was harder to achieve. Twice Turkish foes dumped him out of the Europeans, while a Venezuelan beat him at the worlds – each loss coming in his opening contest – and even victory in the test event before the 2012 Olympics did not earn him selection.

Sean did enjoy a fair amount of success for the British Lionhearts and at multi-nations events before the chance came to extend his Commonwealth supremacy at Glasgow in 2014. First up was a tall Olympian from Australia, Jackson Woods, who led after the first – three judges deciding, following the abandonment of the computer scoring system – but McGoldrick's body punching slowed Woods down and the Newport man went through to the last eight on a split decision.

If anything, it was even closer in the quarter-final, when lanky South African Ayabonga Sonjica's surprise on hearing the announcement of his defeat was shared by many observers, but Sean was guaranteed a medal. It was to be no more than bronze, however, with Ulsterman Michael Conlon clearly in front when a head clash midway through the second left him with a gash above the right eyebrow and forced a premature look at the cards.

Once more there was a clamour for him to ditch the vest, but McGoldrick was in no rush. He did repeat an earlier success at the prestigious Tammer tournament in Finland, but two years went by without too many sightings in the ring. It was something of a relief when he finally made up his mind late in 2016, signing for the expanding stable of Brummie-Irishman Matthew Macklin, with St Joseph's coach Tony Borg still fulfilling the trainer's duty, and made a successful start to his new life among the paid brigade.

BOBBY MORGAN
(1912-1995)

🥊 **Welsh Flyweight Champion 1933-34**

Most valley boxers between the wars juggled their careers with shifts underground. Not Robert Morgan Morgans. His father, Morgan, was an invalid as a result of an accident at the pit, while older brother David worked at the coal face. That was enough.

Instead, Bobby was sent to technical college in Cardiff. Boxing was also something new in the family. The youngest child, he had a harelip and cleft palate and rugby player David, 10 years his senior, taught him the basics so that he could defend himself against schoolyard bullies. Nobody expected him to do it for a living.

After a few amateur bouts, Morgan – the final 's' was somehow mislaid – turned pro and began to cause something of a stir in the heavily populated flyweight division. Victory over former Welsh bantam king Johnny Edmunds saw him matched with Pontypridd prospect Jimmy Jones in an eliminator at the lighter weight.

Ostensibly on neutral ground at Llanelli, Bobby was in effect the "home" fighter, having recently moved to Ammanford to link up with top manager-trainer Johnny Vaughan. It made no difference. While Morgan, who had been ill, earned praise for his speed and intelligent ringcraft, Jimmy's work was generally crisper and cleaner, with greater power in his punches. After 15 rounds, referee C.B. Thomas favoured Jones, much to Vaughan's disgust.

Johnny was in his prime, with no fewer than four Welsh champions in his gym, and, after gaining revenge over Jones on his own patch at Pontypridd, Bobby was to provide him with another. Light-heavy Randy Jones had lost his title eight days earlier, but Morgan restored the stable's dominance by outscoring holder Billy 'Kid' Hughes before a disappointing crowd at Llanelli's Stebonheath Park on July 29, 1933.

Bobby Morgan

The challenger varied his game more and was faster than Hughes, whose cause was further damaged by a propensity to hold. Once he had found the range for his left hand, Bobby was in control, despite shipping the occasional uppercut. Tiredness in the later rounds allowed Billy to chip away at his lead, but there was no doubt about the winner.

The newly crowned champion soon left the Amman Valley to return home, resuming his regular five-mile runs over the hills alongside his collie dog. He began to display his wares across the border, twice losing decisions to former British fly king Bert Kirby, but was struggling with the scales and relinquished his national title to campaign at bantam.

A draw against the unrelated Terence Morgan earned him a Welsh title eliminator with his namesake. They came together in Merthyr, the Aber Valley fighter making the early inroads, and it was not until halfway that Terence, a former national ruler at both fly and bantam, began to show much in the way of positive action. He certainly did enough to close the gap, but – especially given that Bobby clearly won the last – it was something of a shock to the crowd, as well as the loser, when the referee gave his verdict to the man from Tirphil.

There were no further brushes with championship glory as Bobby focussed on earning a crust on the circuit. It was an up-and-down existence, sometimes literally so: Morgan was floored no fewer than seven times during a 10-round points defeat to George Marsden in Leicester, while a trip to Glasgow brought defeat in four by future British and Commonwealth feather boss Johnny McGrory. But he beat former Welsh fly king Charlie Hazel and the useful Al McCoy, while picking up a rare knockout win over Tredegar's Kid Leyland.

He spent time in London, guided by Nat Seller – later to manage Welsh ace Dai Dower – while living in Greenford with some of his Cardiganshire relatives and working on their milk round. But he was back at home by 1939, selling bread from a van and helping out in Caron Caffi, his mother's business in Abertridwr High Street.

A combination of marriage to Marjorie and wartime service as a PTI in the RAF meant an end to his active years in the ring. He settled in the Birchgrove area of Cardiff, working as a delivery driver and passing on his knowledge to the amateurs of the Cardiff Central club.

Despite repeated heart attacks, Bobby lived to the age of 83, long enough to see his grand-daughter, Helen McCrory, take the first steps in her illustrious acting career. A month after his death the BBC screened gritty drama *Streetlife*, which won her BAFTA Cymru's Best Actress award – a second Welsh champion in the family.

DANNY MORGAN
(1896-1942)

🥊 British Featherweight Challenger 1919

Who knows what Danny Morgan might have achieved with less of a thirst? One of the most talented featherweights of his era was pretty successful as it was, despite being the despair of a series of coaches – including the legendary 'Pa' Petersen, father of Jack – who tried in turn to keep him on the straight and narrow.

Many of his fights took place in the cavernous Pavilion Skating Rink at Bargoed, where the boxers used to change in a nearby pub. Inevitably, before heading across to the venue, Danny would prime his pump with a couple of jars.

Once, when he was preparing for an important bout at Hereford, visitors were surprised to hear that he had gone for a run, never an activity he undertook with any enthusiasm. Less than a mile away, they discovered a group of harvesters sharing a barrel of scrumpy with their Welsh guest.

For all his reluctance to train, Danny was always destined to box. After all, his father, 'Dai Rali', had been a fierce combatant on the mountain above Tirphil and made sure that his six sons followed in the family tradition.

Daio was hampered by having just one functioning eye, but still engaged in some 300 scraps. Terence and George each won Welsh titles – and have their own chapters – while Jack reached a final eliminator and the youngest, Reg, was a popular campaigner in the thirties.

By then Danny's race was run. He made his bow as a teenager and by the time he reached 21 he was fighting as far afield as Plymouth, Liverpool and London. He was particularly popular on Merseyside, three times facing former British bantam king Bill Beynon at the old Stadium; the first encounter saw the Taibach man knock out his Welsh rival, but Morgan went back to outpoint Beynon twice over 15 rounds.

There were close battles with Londoner Tommy Noble, another to hold the British bantam title,

Danny Morgan

and when the recently crowned featherweight ruler, Tancy Lee, visited the Rhondda, Danny picked up a 15-round decision – but only after climbing off the canvas three times in the opener.

Morgan was matched with another Lee conqueror, Rhondda boy Billy Fry, to contest the vacant Welsh feather throne at the National Sporting Club on March 4, 1918. It was an event that left the bow-tied members with a poor impression of Welsh boxing; after "a sadly ragged affair" Fry's arm was raised.

But when Billy collapsed in training for a shot at Lee, Danny was invited to occupy the empty stool at the NSC's Covent Garden home on February 24, 1919. Sentimentalists wanted the veteran Lee to achieve the victory that would make him the first Scot to have a Lonsdale Belt to keep. But even they were baffled by the decision that granted them their wish.

Morgan, although troubled by recurrent hand problems – and the fact that the club's bigwigs only sanctioned the bout a few hours earlier – took control from the first bell. With a two-inch height advantage, he dominated at long range, while also controlling the in-fighting, although Lee had his moments, even if Danny blamed an errant elbow for the cut eye he suffered in the ninth.

Tancy, 15 years older than his 22-year-old challenger, tired noticeably after halfway, but remained competitive and arguably shared the final session as a confident Morgan eased off. But the audience were stunned when it was announced that referee John Herbert Douglas favoured Lee. *Boxing* described it as "a miraculous error of judgment", suggesting that Tancy had never looked a winner at any stage. For Danny, such comments were no consolation, although he was still a hero at home, being presented with a gold medal at a banquet in Bargoed to acknowledge his work for war charities.

A trip to Australia – two wins, two losses, two draws – boosted the Tirphil man's bank balance and on his return he set his sights on Welsh lightweight king Billy Moore, from Penygraig, and the pair crossed gloves at Pontypridd's Taff Vale Park on April 18, 1925. While the pair were evenly matched at long range, the harder-hitting Rhondda man was stronger inside, despite Morgan's defensive skills. Danny staged a brave late rally, though it was not enough to deny the "more enterprising" champion on the card of referee Bob Hill.

Morgan later called for a rematch, but it never happened. Indeed, only a few sporadic appearances remained of Danny's career before he officially retired in 1930. His lifestyle began to affect his health and he died of broncho-pneumonia at Merthyr's Tydfil Lodge in 1942. He was only 45.

GEORGE MORGAN
(1913-1981)

🥊 Welsh Featherweight Champion 1934-35

Back in the day it was considered irredeemably posh to have three initials. Valley couples were often accused of social climbing if they merely bestowed a middle name on their offspring. But the people of Tirphil made an exception for David Lloyd George Morgan; he was so christened because he was the first baby in the area whose mother had received maternity benefit under the National Insurance Act pushed through in the Welsh politician's welfare reforms.

Of course, the full handle was just for show. And, given that an older brother was already known as David – or at least 'Daio' – the latest member of the fighting Morgan tribe was generally referred to as George. Keen to follow the family tradition, he was boxing for money soon after his 15th birthday. Naturally, he took time to settle, but he gradually built both a winning streak and a reputation that put him in contention for the Welsh flyweight title.

He was still three days short of 18 when he travelled to Ammanford to meet Swansea's talented Len Beynon in an official eliminator. Beynon was only a year older, but knew far too much for George, taking a clear 15-round decision.

By the time the Rhymney Valley lad reached such exalted heights again, he was a featherweight – and out of his teens. His dedication to training was, like his brothers, questionable, but he was in prime condition when he met ex-bantam king Danny Dando at Bargoed and repeatedly beat the Merthyr man to the punch in a one-sided contest.

George's preparation for another eliminator, against Stan Jehu four months later, was less focussed and, unable to make the weight, he pulled out. The Welsh branch of the Board were not best pleased, but restored him to favour the following year, pairing him with

George Morgan

109

Young Beckett in a final eliminator at Merthyr. Morgan took an early lead against the retreating Rhondda boy and the latter, despite a late surge, was never able to erase the deficit.

Victory earned George a crack at Jehu, by now the champion, but someone the Tirphil fighter had twice outpointed. They met, also in Merthyr, on July 14, 1934, and it proved a thriller. The Maesteg product set the pace, with the challenger content at first to defend and pick him off as he stormed in. Morgan's greater variety and movement saw him into an early lead, but Jehu began to find the range with his left and the fight swung in his favour by the midway stage. George responded, however, his more accurate blows seeing him move clear in the closing sessions to take the decision and the belt.

It was only on loan, however, with Jehu reclaiming his property at Bridgend's Brewery Field on May 25, 1935 – not that everyone agreed with the decision after another cracker. George showed the greater variety of punches, his uppercuts and short lefts to the body proving particularly effective, while Stan's replies lacked power. But Jehu was on the front foot throughout and that may have inclined referee Ben Hardwicke to give him the nod.

Morgan tried again, facing old foe Beynon in a final eliminator in Swansea, but found the wavy-haired wizard too clever and lost a wide decision. The winner moved on to see off Jehu and add the feather crown to his bantam honours, while George returned to the Mannesmann Hall to be knocked out by teenage sensation Ronnie James.

Much of his ability deserted him towards the end, but his enthusiasm was undimmed. The combination of these two elements proved disastrous when he faced Abergavenny puncher Matt Powell in Bargoed. Conceding a stone in weight, George still went charging in, seeking a knockout; scorning defence, he found himself decked four times and halted in the fifth. Other losses were to follow.

As his career petered out, Morgan and his Merthyr-born wife, Mary, moved to Redditch and remained in the West Midlands until his death at the age of 68.

LES MORGAN
(1933-????)

🥊 Welsh Welterweight Champion 1957

Back in the golden days when there was one world champion in each weight division, a Brit travelling to the States to fight for the title was a rarity. When Terry Downes headed for Boston to face Paul Pender in 1961, he was going in with someone who had just claimed back-to-back victories over the legendary Sugar Ray Robinson. The right preparation would be vital.

So the 'Paddington Express' turned for his training partner to a miner's son from Risca. In fact, Les Morgan's accent would have been familiar enough to Downes; he had lived just down the road in Acton since he was nine, learning his boxing in London. He was good enough to win an ABA title and, whisper it, even wore the white vest of England as an amateur.

In his early pro career, Morgan's style was described as "British as the oak tree", but he shocked a few when he added a punch to his repertoire. Perhaps it was a reaction to losing his unbeaten record after eight straight wins, but his next appearance at Wembley Town Hall saw him respond to a two-minute boxing lesson from Eddie Williams by abruptly whipping over a left which dropped the Tredegar man at the end of the first.

Another knockdown in the second and a repeat in the third saw Williams rescued while trapped on the ropes. Manager Jarvis Astaire vowed that he would put Les's name forward for consideration as a contender for the Welsh welter belt worn by another exile, Luton's Rhondda-born Rees Moore.

The match was made, but scrapped when Morgan damaged a hand in training. It was 18 months before he was to get another chance, finally facing Moore on February 18, 1957, at the National Sporting Club's base in the Café Royal, near Piccadilly Circus, ironically far closer to the pair's homes than any venue in Wales would have been. By this stage in his career 34-year-

Les Morgan

old Rees was more clown than combatant; he offered little going forward and relied on distraction as much as deflection when it came to defence. Neither worked.

Four times Les, a decade younger, put the champion on the deck, once in the fourth and twice in the eighth, before another knockdown in the ninth prompted the stoppage. Referee Stanley Davies had lectured Moore four times for various bits of tomfoolery, but the smile had long disappeared from the veteran's face by the climax.

The offers began to flow in, including a date in Marseilles, but with a baby imminent, Les turned everything down to be with his wife, Jean. If life at home was good, things at work began to turn sour.

He was outpointed by a late substitute, Guyana-born Al Browne, in the show-opener of a Harringay bill that, coincidentally, saw the aforementioned Terry Downes win his pro debut in 90 seconds. And at Maindy Stadium – his only appearance in a Welsh ring – Morgan was forced to quit against talented Scot Jimmy Croll after breaking both hands. No workman can continue without the tools of his trade and Les stepped away from the ring.

The urge was still there, however, and three years later he was back in the gym, working with Downes and joining him on his unsuccessful trip to Boston – Pender halted Terry in seven, though the charismatic Cockney dethroned him in a London rematch – before lacing up the gloves on his own account.

The popular Downes was in Morgan's corner at the NSC when he outpointed tough Midlander Terry Banning, but after one more bout it was clear those fragile fists were no better and this time his retirement was final.

TERENCE MORGAN
(1908-1966)

🥊 **Welsh Flyweight Champion 1928**

🥊 **Welsh Bantamweight Champion 1931-32**

Any son of mountain fighter Dai Morgan was destined for the ring, and, in accordance with family expectations, Terence turned pro at 16, soon cutting a swathe through his local rivals. There was the occasional defeat, but these were usually reversed in rematches. Yet there was one rival the latest Morgan off the Tirphil production line found particularly stubborn.

Ginger Williams, from Bedwas, despite a mediocre record, enjoyed facing Terence. Two points victories and a draw underlined the fact. But when they were reunited with the vacant Welsh flyweight throne at stake, things proved different.

Morgan had already had one shot at a national title, of sorts. He took on former victim Billy 'Kid' Hughes for the unofficial championship at paperweight, knocking him out with a body blow in the 12th of their scheduled 20-rounder at Pill Labour Hall, Newport. The referee completed the count, but then invited the doctor to examine the stricken Maesteg man; when the medic found evidence of a low blow, Terence was disqualified.

There was no such controversy when he faced Williams at the same venue on April 8, 1928, with a sidestake of £25 adding flavour to the occasion. Terence began at a high pace and it took Williams a good half-dozen rounds to settle, doing well at close quarters, where his heavier shots seemed to have some effect. Morgan tired, but kept his left in Ginger's face often enough to discourage him and guarantee the decision after a gripping encounter.

The fight coincided with the formation of a Welsh Board, and, presumably wanting to establish their authority, they told Terence he had to take part in a set of eliminators intended to decide a new, officially sanctioned ruler. His first foe was Rhondda namesake Freddie, who proceeded to drop him in the fourth with a body punch. Some pundits had suggested that Terence – by now living in Newport – would struggle to maintain a high workrate;

Terence Morgan

113

Terence proudly parades his Welsh belt

he proved them wrong and took a wide victory. But he pulled out of the tournament, watching Pentre's Phineas John, a man he had beaten, succeed to "his" title. Terence had his sights on bigger prizes.

Twice he drew with Londoner Ernie Jarvis, just back from a stint in North America which included a world title challenge, and then sailed to Australia, where he won a few, but drew and lost against Commonwealth bantam king Billy McAllister. It was in the heavier division that Terence was to campaign on his return.

British fly champion Bert Kirby was given an ovation when he stepped into the ring for a catchweight bout at Pontypridd's Taff Vale Park, but found Morgan less respectful, dropping him twice with body shots, the second of which was not merely downstairs, but in the basement; with Kirby in agony, disqualification was inevitable.

Morgan took British and Commonwealth bantam boss Teddy Baldock to a tight decision at the Blackfriars Ring and returned to the domestic scene with confidence. Welsh bantam ruler Stan Jehu was widely regarded as there to be taken and Terence made no mistake at Pontypridd on June 22, 1931. There was little between them for the first third of the fight, but Morgan's piercing left then helped him into a wide lead. The Llynfi Valley man had some joy at close quarters, while he rallied in the closing sessions, but there was no doubt about the winner.

The Welsh Board warned Terence, who had not taken out a licence since that body affiliated to the new British authority, that unless he rectified the situation within a week, he would be stripped of his crown. The paperwork duly sorted out, he put his belt on the line at Merthyr on June 11, 1932, against the high-flying Swansea lad, Len Beynon.

Without a win in six fights – including a points loss to Beynon in London – few expected Morgan to survive the challenge. And he produced a patchy performance, good rounds being followed by poor, while Beynon boxed consistently well after a slow start. His ability to draw Terence's leads and counter to the body slowly sapped the strength of the Tirphil man and although the latter staged a late revival, it was never enough to prevent the crown changing hands.

There was one more bid for glory. Morgan edged an eliminator victory over Abertridwr namesake Bobby, but faded against the younger Mog Mason to miss the chance of regaining his title from Beynon. Next time out Terence was halted by former victim Jehu and the decline in his fortunes proved irreversible. By the time World War II broke out, he had already declared his own ceasefire.

Terence (left) and brother George out with their dogs

TOMMY MORGAN
(1898-1941)

🥊 **Welsh Lightweight Champion 1922-24**

L ike most youngsters in the heady excitement of World War I, Thomas John Morgan wanted to "do his bit". But the Blaenavon youngster was a miner, and even after conscription was introduced in 1916, his work underground was considered more important than soldiering. It was May 1918 before the 19-year-old received the call, serving just five months as an artilleryman in Derby before being discharged.

If he missed out on the fighting in France, Tommy made up for it in the ring. Naturally, most of his early action came close to home, but he soon proved himself a decent scrapper and began to attract attention from the other side of Offa's Dyke.

He enjoyed success in Liverpool and Manchester, while on home ground, a string of victories placed him as an outstanding contender for the Welsh lightweight title. The ageing champion, Tirphil's Arthur Evans, had been singularly unwilling to respond to the clamour from would-be opponents, but was eventually persuaded to defend against Morgan.

Even then there were disputes over dates and venues before the duo came together on March 20, 1922, at the Market Hall, Blackwood. The 38-year-old holder was in charge in the early rounds, Tommy biding his time and keeping clear of Arthur's renowned punch. But, inevitably, Evans began to slow, at which point the challenger, younger by 15 years, took the initiative. Twice the veteran was floored before his corner surrendered for him in the 11th. The king is dead, long live the king!

While Evans's story was at an end, his successor was inundated with challenges from all those left in the cold by the previous ruler's inactivity. But then as now there were plenty of reasons why touted showdowns never actually happened.

Injuries were always a bugbear. As well as regular hand problems, there was a broken nose which required surgery and sidelined him for three months. In addition, the champion's camp were looking upwards and, after lengthy negotiations, Seaman 'Nobby' Hall, the British and European lightweight boss, agreed to face him at the Drill Hall in Cardiff on March 5, 1923.

Hall and his manager, Ted Broadribb, made sure the contract allowed the

Tommy Morgan

Scot to scale two pounds over the divisional limit, thus protecting his titles should anything untoward occur. After the 20 rounds, fought out before a packed house, they were no doubt congratulating themselves on their foresight.

Morgan, slightly taller and speedier of foot, shaded the early sessions, although Hall stepped up the pace later. The sailor also began to mark up as a result of Tommy's attentions, but there was little between them at the end. Referee Charles Barnett's nod towards Morgan brought a furious response from the visitors. Broadribb followed up with a complaint to *Boxing*, rebutted the next week by Tommy's manager, D.W. Davies, invoking support from the likes of Freddie Welsh.

Davies claimed that Broadribb had promised a rematch with the belts at stake, but Hall instead took on Leeds wannabe Harry Mason and lost the title when he was turfed out for low blows; Morgan had to look elsewhere. He climbed off the deck to outscore former British feather king Mike Honeyman, but both hands went again. Then a damaged ear forced the cancellation of a meeting with Ernie Rice, once British and European lightweight boss. Meanwhile, Rhondda publican Billy Moore had been patiently awaiting his shot at Tommy's Welsh title and the pair finally met at Pontypool's Crane Street Cinema on March 31, 1924.

The champion's rust was obvious. He could not find his rhythm on a night which disappointed the large contingent who had travelled down from Blaenavon, with Moore keeping his long left in Morgan's face. Billy was also useful on the inside and while there was never a lot between them even the home fans accepted the justice of the decision that sent the crown to Penygraig.

When Tommy faced Rice, now trained by Cardiffian Fred Dyer, the value of good conditioning was made clear to the National Sporting Club members as Ernie floored Morgan 10 times en route to a sixth-round stoppage.

Recurrent injuries prompted repeated pull-outs: on one occasion, Morgan turned up for the weigh-in for a rematch with namesake Danny, waited until the crowd had arrived at the Pontypridd venue – and then cried off. Such antics did nothing for his reputation with promoters and punters alike.

The problem with his hands was real enough, though. A London specialist had no answers, so D.W. advised his charge to hang up his gloves. He reappeared from time to time, losing a welter eliminator to old foe Moore and basing himself in London for a spell, but it was pretty much all over.

There was a spell coaching airmen at an RAF base in Lincolnshire, but Tommy ended up working on building sites to earn a crust. It was on one such job in the Midlands that he died following an accident at the age of 42.

MO NASIR
(1986-)

🥊 Commonwealth Games Bronze Medallist 2006

For a youngster of Yemeni heritage growing up in Britain in the nineties, there was only one sporting hero to follow. And it was the example set by Naseem Hamed that inspired 10-year-old Mohammed Abdul-Wahab Nasir to lace up the gloves at Newport's St Joseph's gym.

Mo lived around the corner in the Pill district, having arrived two years earlier to join his father, who had moved to Newport to work as a welder. And coach Tony Borg soon realised he had a special talent on his hands.

Welsh titles at schools and cadets levels were accompanied by a Four Nations gold – another was lost to future world champion Jamie McDonnell. Domestic dominance was repeated when Nasir graduated to the senior ranks, three Welsh ABA championships and a further Four Nations triumph paving the way to the international scene.

Appearances in Europe and further afield brought some early competition exits – hardly surprising for a teenager – but a few trips to the podium as well. Success at the prestigious Tammer tournament was accompanied by the Best Boxer award, while Ulsterman Paddy Barnes, who would go on to win two Olympic medals, was beaten en route to a Commonwealth Federation gold.

That event, in Glasgow, was merely the appetiser for the Commonwealth Games proper in Melbourne in 2006. The draw hardly favoured Nasir, who was one of a handful of light-flyweights to miss out on a first-round bye. Instead, he had to overcome Kenyan southpaw Peter Warui, a task he achieved by 22-17 on the computer scoring system, Mo's skill and mobility proving the difference.

Mo Nasir with his Commonwealth Federation gold

Next up was Ghanaian Manyo Plange, who had halted a Tanzanian in his prelim bout, but posed fewer problems for Nasir, the Welshman earning a clear-cut 27-12 score. And the same margin – actually 30-15 – saw him past near-namesake Muhammad Nisar, of Pakistan, constantly changing his angles and firing in uppercuts to underline his superiority.

The three victories guaranteed Mo a medal, but the semi-final brought him up against Englishman Darran Langley, runner-up four years earlier in Manchester. Things began well, Nasir edging the first two rounds, but the Londoner took command in the third, staying on the outside and making the Newport youngster miss. Even an increased workrate in the fourth and final session was not enough to prevent Mo going down by 19-13 and having to settle for bronze.

After a countback loss to Langley at the following year's EU championships, Nasir moved up to flyweight and set his sights on the Beijing Olympics, but injury shattered his dreams. After seeing off a Romanian at the Roseto qualifying tournament, Mo faced a familiar face from the Sheffield-based GB squad, Khalid Yafai, who was representing England.

But an ankle problem sustained in training forced him to retire mid-contest, leaving Yafai, coincidentally also of Yemeni descent, to fill the seat on the plane for China. Nasir, whose injury kept him sidelined for four months, decided to turn pro, but that ambition was also to be dashed. The Board's compulsory brain scan showed an anomaly and the medics, although unsure whether it presented a danger, were unwilling to take a risk.

But things have turned out for the best, despite the initial frustration. Turning his attention to training, he is now the proud boss at Mo's Boxing and Fitness Academy in Pill's Alexandra Road.

DAVID PEARCE
(1959-2000)

British Heavyweight Champion 1983-1985

European Heavyweight Challenger 1984

Boxers were getting bigger. The likes of Rocky Marciano and Joe Louis scaled less than 14st for most of their careers; the same with Joe Erskine in Wales. But by the 1970s a new breed of heavyweights were taking over, regularly weighing a couple of stone more. So the powers-that-be came up with a new division. They called it cruiserweight.

The World Boxing Council introduced their first title at 13st 8lb in 1979. Over the next four years the WBA and IBF followed suit. But like most innovations in the fight game, it took time for the essentially conservative British Board of Control to fall in line. Until 1985, in fact, by which time it was too late for David Pearce.

One of seven sons born to former booth fighter Wally – six boxed professionally – David was the brightest star in the family firmament. His father, realising he had a gem on his hands, took him to a master: the legendary Eddie Thomas shaped and polished the raw material in his Penydarren gym before launching him on the pro scene shortly after his 19th birthday.

His usual nickname, 'Yucker', was replaced by the more militant 'Bomber' and Pearce made his bow in the semi-final of a heavyweight competition organised by his manager on a charity show at Merthyr's Rhydycar Sports Centre. The new boy floored Nottingham novice Osborne Taylor twice and stopped him in 38 seconds.

David, a former steelworker who used his redundancy money to pay for training trips to the US, introduced himself to a London audience and earned a £2,000 cheque for winning one of Jack Solomons's novice tournaments at the World Sporting Club. When Thomas staged his own final, the Newport teenager floored Cardiffian Winston

David Pearce

Pearce batters British champion Meade

Allen, but had to settle for points before banking another grand.

A seventh-round stoppage of former Southern Area champion Denton Ruddock indicated a move up in class, suggesting that he would dethrone Welsh heavyweight king Neville Meade – who had been halted by Ruddock – when they met at Caerphilly's Club Double Diamond on January 22, 1980. But the form line proved misleading. Pearce, conceding two and a half stone, seemed overawed in the opener and was floored early in the second. He was hanging on under severe pressure when referee Jim Brimmell called a halt 12 seconds before the end of the session.

But the Newport lad rebounded with five straight successes, including a seventh-round win over future world light-heavy boss Dennis Andries (whose pro debut was against David's brother Ray at Newport's Stowaway Club) and a fifth-round knockout of Gordon Ferris in a final eliminator for the British title taken off the Ulsterman by that man Meade.

Pearce was now managed by Burt McCarthy, a self-made millionaire with an Essex mansion and a stuck-down comb-over, and, perhaps recalling their first meeting – and the difference in size – it was decided to reject a shot at the Lonsdale Belt and seek opportunities abroad in the new cruiserweight class. But they found little encouragement from the Board and in the end the rematch with Meade went ahead, top promoter Mike Barrett staging it at the new St David's Hall in Cardiff on September 22, 1983. British title fights had just been reduced to 12 rounds, but contracts for this scrap had been signed before the change, so it was the last to go ahead as a 15-rounder. Most thought the scheduled distance would be academic.

Meade had paid uncharacteristic attention to training and this time was only a stone heavier than the challenger. He watched calmly as David bounced about the ring during the formalities. Some wondered if the challenger's exuberance indicated an inner nervousness, but they were soon disabused of that theory: while Neville controlled the early exchanges with his left lead, Pearce blocked most blows heading his way and absorbed what did get through without apparent distress.

David shows off the Lonsdale Belt at Somerton Park, just yards from his home

A fourth-round uppercut from Meade resulted in no more than a grin from David, who gradually began to force the champion into reverse. A dozen years older, the Swansea man began to look it as Pearce drove him into a corner in the seventh. Neville hurled a last-hurrah right to the chin in the eighth, but its recipient merely turned to the crowd and laughed; disheartened, Meade took a step back, slipped on wet canvas in his corner and was dropped by a swift right before he could regain his balance.

The ninth brought the official passing of the torch. David waited for a last desperate assault to fade before ripping in a perfect left hook which left Neville slumped across the ropes; referee Roland Dakin leapt between them and the veteran's reign was over.

The new ruler was promptly nominated to take on European champion Lucien Rodriguez in Limoges on March 30, 1984. A night, bizarrely, spent on a park bench, coupled with damage to both hands, were not the best preparation to face Moroccan-born Rodriguez, who had gone the full 12 rounds in a WBC challenge to Larry Holmes. He was making the sixth defence of his second reign and, apart from a rocky eighth round, it proved among the easiest.

Giving away height and reach, eight pounds in weight and a world in experience, David constantly marched forward even though his cross-armed defence was ineffectual in keeping the skilful Frenchman at bay. The ring was the largest permissible and Lucien used it well, making his foe miss badly, while bringing blood from the Welshman's nose.

A cut alongside Rodriguez's left eye inspired Pearce to greater efforts and in the eighth two solid rights dropped the surprised champion on the seat of his pants. Stunned, he rose at four for the mandatory eight, but was swiftly bundled over once more; after a seemingly slow count, prompting angry protests from manager McCarthy, Lucien kept on the move until the safety of the bell.

David's chance was gone. Lucien regained control and the Newport fighter's brave aggression made no further dents in his armour. All three judges voted for the champion; Pearce had to settle for a standing ovation from fans who appreciated his courage and determination.

There was a bigger blow to come. A routine brain scan back in 1982 had provoked concern but, after consultation with a Harley Street neurologist, David had been cleared to box on. Another check, prior to the European bid, also suggested problems, but the Board nevertheless allowed him to face Rodriguez. When he returned from France he found that following further discussion, the ruling body had decided to pull his licence.

The newly introduced MRI test, showing greater detail than the CT scan then generally in use, revealed he had a cyst – and that it had grown, although it could not be said with certainty whether boxing had played a part. The arguments became academic when the Board announced that new regulations would prevent them licensing anyone with an abnormality of the brain, however caused. Despite thousands spent on legal and medical fees, Pearce had to accept defeat.

But he still wanted to box. The Board's reputation worldwide meant no established authority would ignore their decision, but still David kept searching. Eventually, he was granted a permit by the Ohio Commission in the US and, more than six years after his previous action, climbed through the ropes in a Michigan hotel to face the obese Percell Davis. A shadow of his old self, David was embarrassingly beaten in seven rounds. It was a sad way to end a fine career.

In later years he developed epilepsy and a form of Alzheimer's, but still helped found Alway amateur club. Shortly after his 41st birthday, he died at home.

The Alway ABC gym on Liswerry Road is now the David Pearce Memorial Hall, while a statue is planned for the city centre as a further symbol of Newport's love for its much missed champion.

GARY PEARCE
(1960-)

🥊 **Welsh Light-Middleweight Champion 1981-84**

The fact that the fifth of the fighting Pearce brothers appears on the honours board at 11st is something of an anomaly. Gary was a welterweight for most of his career and had only scaled above that division's limit once – and that by just half a pound.

But you take your chance when it is offered. And the 20-year-old from Pill made no mistake when he was whistled up as a late replacement for fellow-townsman Richard Avery to challenge for the vacant Welsh light-middle throne at Tiffany's Ballroom, Newport, on April 7, 1981.

Unlike Pearce, his opponent, Swansea banger Terry Matthews, had to shed a pound and threequarters at the lunchtime weigh-in – he managed it by skipping for 45 minutes in a sweatsuit borrowed from Gary's brother, David – and his lack of preparation showed. The local boy took a couple of sessions to check the lie of the land, but began to counter the forward-moving Matthews, whose nose bled from early on.

There was little Terry could do to change the one-sided nature of the exchanges and came under steady fire in the eighth. When referee Jim Brimmell realised that the same scenario was being played out in the ninth, he stepped between them and raised Pearce's arm as the champion of a class in which he had never before boxed.

Gary's reputation for providing entertainment was born in his pro debut, a draw with Deptford's Billy O'Grady which saw both men down and brought a shower of "nobbings" from a National Sporting Club crowd which had frequently broken the institution's rule about remaining silent during the rounds.

A light-welter in his early days under Dai Gardiner, Gary suffered his first loss in Birmingham when he was edged out by newcomer Lloyd Hibbert, later to win British and Commonwealth belts up at light-middle. It was the only reverse in his opening 11 bouts, during which he ended the seven-fight winning streak of Cardiffian Alan Burrows and added Swansea's Frank McCord and Llantwit Major's Dil Collins to his list of Welsh victims.

Gary Pearce

Gary (left) in a pre-fight chat with fellow-townsman Richard Avery

His form earned a crack at the Welsh welter throne, occupied by Jamaican-born Horace McKenzie, like Gary one of a band of boxing brothers. They met on neutral ground – though familiar to both – at the NSC's Café Royal headquarters on March 11, 1980. Pearce bundled McKenzie to the canvas in the sixth and was the cleaner puncher throughout a fairly untidy encounter, but his slow start meant that third man Brimmell had the holder half a point up at the final bell.

Hopes of a rematch were dashed when Gary, still only 19, was outscored by Ringland pipe-fitter Avery in an eliminator at Tiffany's. But instead of challenging McKenzie, Richard was matched with Matthews, only to be forced out by hand and elbow injuries which meant he never boxed again. Young Pearce had the call to step in and wrote his name in the record books.

Ironically, it was the last time Gary boxed in Wales. His first outing as champion brought a points victory over Ghanaian Tony Martey, but there was only one more cause for celebration in his final 11 contests.

The defeats came against some decent operators. Pearce floored Danish idol Hans-Henrik Palm before losing an eight-round decision in Copenhagen, but future British and Commonwealth king Sylvester Mittee and former British and European light-welter ruler Colin Power each halted the Welshman. Called up from the crowd as a late, late substitute, Gary, in borrowed gear, held highly rated Londoner Gary Knight to a half-point margin.

But after two-time British welter challenger Rocky Kelly knocked him out in two, Pearce handed back his Welsh crown, a week before he was due to defend against Swansea's John McGlynn.

He reappeared after a two-year gap and lost over eight rounds to Amman Valley-Irishman Terry Magee, but when stocky Gloucester man Johnny Williamson blitzed him inside a round it marked the end of the line, apart from a few outings on the unlicensed circuit.

The boxing brothers – Bimbo, Ray, Ron and David at rear; Gary and Nigel in front

GEORGE PEMBRIDGE
(1891-1967)

Welsh Middleweight Champion 1920

The market town of Monmouth gave birth to a great warrior in King Henry V, the victor of Agincourt. But it has never been renowned for producing champions in the ring – with one exception.

George Henry Pembridge was raised in Chippenhamgate Street, running down to the River Wye, one of a large family born to Charles, a tiler and plasterer. Young George did not follow his father's profession, instead becoming a butcher, while seeking a few extra bob with his fists, as did kid brother Jim.

"Tall, swarthy, with good reach and typical fighting face," according to a contemporary observer, Pembridge began to make an impression locally and soon introduced himself to a wider audience.

In those days a boxer had to audition to appear at the august National Sporting Club; George passed the test before returning to outbox experienced Scot Johnny Matheson, the reporter from *Boxing* urging its readers to keep an eye on him.

The Welshman went from high society to the other end of boxing's social scale and dazzled the knowledgeable fans at Liverpool Stadium by swiftly dispatching visiting American Kid Johnson. But the war brought an abrupt halt to his progress. He reached the rank of sergeant and won a divisional tournament in France, but his pro career as such was on hold for five years.

The first key contest on his return saw him face Welsh rugby international Jerry Shea at the Drill Hall on Newport's Stow Hill, with a silver challenge cup at stake. George's preparations were hit by flu, while his nose was broken early on as Shea demonstrated the full range of his skills to run out a clear winner after 15 rounds. Yet it

George Pembridge

was Pembridge who found himself contesting the Welsh middleweight title in his next outing, on January 31, 1920.

At another Drill Hall, this time over the border in Hereford, George, a familiar figure there, started strongly, with defending champion Harry Davies seemingly content to box on the retreat. The challenger was able to build a decent lead, but Caerau's Davies, a Welsh titleholder in the amateur ranks as well, increased his efforts and narrowed the gap between them. It was anyone's fight going into the final session, but Pembridge caught the eye and referee Bill Bevan handed him a popular verdict.

George's reign was not to be a long one. Even though the belt was not at stake when he was outpointed by Aberavon veteran Will Brooks over 15 rounds at Bargoed – a verdict which sparked a riot, with the referee flattened in the mayhem – it was up for grabs just three weeks later, on July 24, 1920, at Llanelli's Stradey Park. Local hero Shoeing-Smith Fred Davies had just left the Army and returned to Wales, calling out all the local middleweights; Pembridge was the first to respond, but perhaps regretted his enthusiasm.

Though nearly half a stone heavier, the holder was not fully fit, looking slow and sluggish. From the fourth round he began to tire, and Davies – later to become a publican in Pembridge's native Monmouth – floored him in the fifth and the ninth. When George went down again three times in the 12th, Newport referee Llew Morgan called a halt, just as the towel floated in.

One week on – no suspensions back then – Pembridge faced Brooks again at the Abertillery Palladium, only to retire after four rounds with a shoulder injury. There were to be few successes in the declining years of George's career, although he did climb off the deck twice to last 15 rounds with the fast-rising Pontypridd lad, Frank Moody, on his way to becoming a two-weight British champion.

Future world title challenger Ted Moore, from Plymouth, was among those who stopped Pembridge, now a light-heavy, in the last knockings of his career. Defeat inside 10 rounds to Rhondda policeman Emy Thomas underlined George's decline and he slid into retirement, moving to Porthcawl, where he earned a crust as a lifeguard on the resort's beaches. The man old-timers called 'Corbett', seeing a resemblance to the former world heavyweight king, never married, living to the age of 75.

DICK POWER
(1903-????)

Welsh Heavyweight Champion 1926-32

As a name for a fighter, Dick Power has to be up there with Johnny Basham. Ironically, the valleys policeman was never noted as a big puncher, but nevertheless ruled the roost in Wales for six years.

Brought up in Gelli Houses, Tredegar, his impact was delayed by four years in the South Wales Borderers, but he wasted no time after returning to civvy street. With Shoeing-Smith Fred Davies taking care of the training side and Fred's own manager and fellow Monmouth publican D.W. Davies pulling the strings, Power laid down a marker by outpointing former Welsh heavy king Trevor Llewellyn over the border at Lydney and raised eyebrows in London when Belgian Pierre Charles – later a three-time European champion – was pulled out after two minutes.

A cracking fight at Crumlin's Palace Theatre on Boxing Day 1925 saw Dick go down somewhat unluckily to Tom Norris. The Rhondda boy had been inactive, but the pair maintained a tremendous pace for big men. Dick had built a substantial lead when a clubbing right from Norris split his left eyebrow; at the end of the round, the referee had a close look and waved it off, a decision backed by the loser's manager.

Although involving arguably the best two heavyweights in Wales, this could not be considered a title fight as it was only scheduled for 15 rounds. But the throne was up for grabs when they met again before a record crowd at Taff Vale Park, near Pontypridd, on April 5, 1926. This time Power's aggression prevailed over Norris's defensive skills, but only after Dick had been decked twice. A blow beneath the heart in the seventh saw him take a count of seven, but he rose immediately from a further knockdown and stayed in control to the final bell.

After avenging the Norris loss, Power used his reach advantage to outpoint Yorkshireman Harry Crossley, despite an early cut. Crossley went on to win the British light-heavy title, but the man who beat him announced his retirement to join Monmouthshire Police.

Dick Power

Power (left) weighs in for his brief clash with Jack Petersen

He reappeared in the summer of 1928, but the next few years saw Crossley gain his revenge, while future British ruler Reggie Meen finished Dick in two rounds, leaving the Gwent fighter with no illusions about his position in the pecking order.

Power saw off London-based George Smith, originally from Tonyrefail, at Merthyr to secure a lucrative defence against the fast-rising Jack Petersen. The 8,000 who packed Cardiff's Greyfriars Hall on February 3, 1932, may not have had much for their money, but nobody complained. When the bell sounded, the tall, handsome local, still only 20 and a pro for less than five months, walked to the centre of the ring, hurled a left to Power's temple and immediately followed it with a right to the body. Dick stepped back, but Jack was straight on him, rocking the policeman with a left to the jaw and adding a thunderous right which sent the champion flying backwards, his head thumping into the boards.

The young prodigy calmly stood, his arms along the ropes, as the count was completed and then went to check on his rival before turning to celebrate with his trainer-father. Not everyone shared their joy: one Power cornerman illustrated his frustration with a blow to the nose of the senior Petersen, but 'Pa' merely laughed and the sore loser slunk away.

The winner would claim Lonsdale Belts at both light-heavy and heavy within the next five months, but his victim disappeared from the scene. There were two further bouts, six years later, when the 34-year-old lost a decision to the even older Gipsy Daniels, but finished with a win against another veteran, South African Don McCorkindale.

His police career came to an ignominious end in 1943. Sergeant Power was found to be frequenting a drinking club at Cwmfelinfach, of which, crucially, he was not a member, therefore technically breaking the law. Dick was told he would be reduced to constable; he declined the offer and was promptly kicked out of the force.

He was 'mine host' at a Hertford hostelry for a few years before emigrating to New South Wales in 1949 with his wife and three youngest children, settling in Newcastle and working in the local steelworks before reverting to the pub trade.

LAUREN PRICE
(1994-)

🥊 **Commonwealth Games Bronze Medallist 2014**

🥊 **European Bronze Medallist 2011, 2016**

🥊 **World Youth Bronze Medallist 2011**

The girl from Bargoed could have found athletic success in any number of disciplines – indeed, she already had. But it was boxing which brought her to wider public attention, when she claimed Wales's first Commonwealth medal in the female side of the sport.

When her grandfather took 10-year-old Lauren Price to the gym to keep fit, it was kick-boxing and football which grabbed her interest. Two years later she claimed the first of her four world titles in the former, while the latter soon saw her snapped up by Cardiff City. She also managed to fit in netball, where she represented her country at Under-14 level.

There was another change of direction when Lauren answered a call for those with a potential talent for taekwondo, seeing off 2,000 rivals, but that meant basing herself in Manchester – where she shared a house with future double Olympic champion Jade Jones – and homesickness eventually prompted her to return home and focus on boxing.

Her ability was immediately obvious: after only one bout, the 16-year-old was picked to represent Wales at the World Youth Championships in Turkey and returned with a bronze medal. It might have been more, as she lost the semi-final on injury against the Swede who went on to win gold.

Six months later she matched it with another at the European senior event at Rotterdam, seeing off rivals from Ireland

Lauren Price with her Commonwealth bronze

Lauren in football action for Wales

and Turkey before losing to experienced Ukrainian Maria Badulina.

Already a regular in the Wales football squad, Price turned her back on a World Cup qualifying campaign to concentrate on preparing for the 2014 Commonwealth Games, where women's boxing would make its first appearance. The sacrifice proved worthwhile.

Her first outing in Glasgow came against a 19-year-old Guyanese, Theresa London, who looked like a rabbit caught in the headlights, barely landing a blow and taking two standing counts as Lauren danced her way to a whitewash points win.

The quarter-final pitted the Welsh woman against blonde Australian Kaye Scott, who had little to offer as Price picked her off with southpaw right crosses. In the fourth, the Moroccan referee gave Scott two standing counts before the Sydneysider landed a solid right in the last 10 seconds and he opted to toll eight in front of the temporarily embarrassed Price as well. No matter, it was a clear, unanimous decision and a medal was secure.

Next up was 29-year-old Canadian Ariane Fortin, a two-time world gold medallist who had outpointed Lauren when they met during the Welsh squad's pre-Games warm-up trip to Regina in May. A foregone conclusion then? Not a bit of it!

The Welsh hope began superbly, flicking out effective right leads as her fellow southpaw moved in, taking the first on all cards and the second on two. But as she tired Fortin began to land more often and Price had to take a standing count late in the third, tipping the round the Canadian's way. The fourth was an intense affair, both scoring with solid shots before the Uzbek referee leapt in just as the final bell sounded to hand Lauren another count, completed as she had her gloves loosened by national coach Colin Jones.

The scoring reflected how hard the bout was to judge, one judge seeing Price three points clear and another favouring Fortin by the same margin.

The third arbiter – a Brazilian named Jones, would you believe – had the pair level, but gave his decisive vote to the Canadian.

A trip later that year to the world championships on the South Korean island of Jeju saw Lauren lost her first bout on a 2-1 majority decision to Panamanian Atheyna Bylon – she went on to strike gold – but she claimed a top scalp at a multi-nations at Cartagena, Spain, when she followed up victory over the local representative with a split-decision verdict over Commonwealth champion Savannah Marshall. But the final saw the Welsh girl on the wrong end of a split, the judges favouring Russian Yaroslava Yakushina.

There was a gold medal to take home from Rotherham later in the month, however. Unanimous decisions over English pair Stephanie Wroe and Paige Murney earned Price a GB gold, matched by team-mates Lynsey Holdaway and Charlene Jones on an outstanding weekend for Welsh women. Another gold came at the Queen's Cup in Germany, with victories over a local girl and a Finn followed by split decisions over England's Stacey Copeland and Russian Darima Sandakova.

Lauren had to settle for silver up at middleweight at the 2016 Three Nations in Scotland, losing a split decision to England's Natasha Gale despite forcing the action throughout.

She came up against Gale again back at the Queen's Cup and this time made no mistake, taking a unanimous decision and another gold medal. But when the rivals found themselves paired in the semi-finals of the European championships in Bulgaria, Lauren, who had seen off a Pole to reach that stage, found Gale too good and had to settle for bronze, while her English nemesis went on to take the main prize.

A few days before Christmas 2016, Lauren received the perfect present, a call inviting her to join the GB podium potential squad and take aim at the Tokyo Olympics. In 2017 another Welsh title was followed by a Three Nations gold on home ground at the Sport Wales National Centre in Cardiff, when she overcame two questionable warnings to outscore a former victim, tall English soldier Wroe.

Next up for Price is another Commonwealth Games, on Australia's Gold Coast. Another medal would be very welcome!

BRADLEY PRYCE
(1981-)

- Commonwealth Light-Middleweight Champion 2006-09

- Commonwealth Middleweight Challenger 2012

- European Light-Middleweight Challenger 2013

- British Welterweight Challenger 2003, 2005

- Welsh Welterweight Champion 2004-06

- WBO Inter-Continental Lightweight Champion 2001-02

- IBF Inter-Continental Light-Welterweight Champion 2002

Booze and burgers were the two toughest opponents in the Newbridge fighter's long career. He had the talent to overcome most rivals, but the scales were always a different matter.

Bradley Pryce

Ironically, as an amateur it was a lack of weight that made him stand out. When he followed a British schools title with Welsh ABA success as a senior, it was at featherweight – and, at an inch south of six foot, that was borderline freakish.

Still 18 when he followed brothers Byron and Delroy in turning pro – Frank Warren did the deals, while amateur mentor Enzo Calzaghe looked after training – 'Sugar Sweet' proceeded to win his first 16, picking up the WBO Inter-Continental lightweight belt with a points verdict over Londoner Jason Hall and defending against South African Lucky Sambo before adding the IBF version up at light-welter with a stoppage victory over Gavin Down memorable for the fact that brother Byron, seeking a closer view, dropped from the York Hall balcony and broke a leg. He then insisted on watching the fight before being taken to hospital!

There was talk of an autumn shot at British 10st champion Junior Witter, but disaster struck on a summer evening in the open air at Cardiff Castle, when Zaire-born Londoner Ted Bami halted Pryce just one second before the bell to end their six-rounder. When he returned to knock out fragile Midlander Colin Lynch three months later, Bradley was over the light-middle limit.

The Punching Pryces - Byron, Delroy and Bradley

But a British title opportunity did come his way, at welterweight, where Ulsterman Neil Sinclair clinched a Lonsdale Belt to keep when he halted Pryce in eight in Belfast. The Welshman bounced back with a brilliant display to outpoint previously unbeaten Russian Ivan Kirpa at Widnes, only to be sidelined until he completed a spell of community service following a court appearance for assault, a ban which stymied a planned challenge to WBU light-middle king Takaloo.

He reappeared as a fleshy middleweight and was outpointed by Zimbabwean journeyman Farai Musiyiwa – perhaps the low point of his career – before slimming to light-middle and losing another decision to traveller Thomas McDonagh for the lightly regarded WBU International strap.

Bradley managed to make welter to claim the vacant Welsh throne with an eighth-round stoppage of willing warrior Keith Jones – a rare Welsh title fight promoted by Warren – but his next outing at the Newport Centre saw him despatched in four by unbeaten Nigerian Ajose Olusegun. Another man with a 100 per cent record, Russian Sergei Stepkin, was halted in the last of 10, however, and Pryce found himself facing British ruler Michael Jennings at Preston Guild Hall on October 25, 2005. There was a shock when the Welshman dropped Jennings in the first, but the Chorley man took over to claim a unanimous decision.

When he was given a shot at Ghanaian Ossie Duran for the Commonwealth light-middle title, he regarded it as a one-off. "It's not a weight I want to be staying at," he said in the lead-up to the bout. Then he won – and held the title for three years. The victory had been unexpected, but regular texts from Joe Calzaghe, fresh from his stunning defeat of Jeff Lacy, drove home the message that, if he boxed, Bradley was a match for anyone. At

Pryce (right) has Ossie Duran covering up on the way to the Commonwealth title

the Newport Centre on March 11, 2006, Pryce proved the point.

Duran was a hot favourite, having beaten all eight British opponents, including a three-round knockout of Jamie Moore, and the first session underlined his quality, two rights rocking the Gwent man, who was cut on the nose and near an eye by the end of the third. But Bradley scored well at close range in the fourth and ended the session with a left which wobbled the champion, totally changing their respective mindsets.

Pryce stepped up the pace, firing fast combinations, while Ossie began to stand off and cede the initiative. He was never to regain it and the Newbridge fighter romped home, the judge from Accra having his countryman a full six points in arrears.

The new king – now father to two girls and less inclined to party – soon settled into his role, seeing off no fewer than six challengers. There were two more Africans, Tanzanian Hassan Matumla and Ghanaian Thomas Awinbono, both beaten at the Millennium Stadium, while four English rivals also came up short. Lanky Sheffielder Andrew Facey was outpointed in Newport, cocky Cockney Anthony Small – later to become a militant Islamist – and Midlanders Martin Concepcion and Marcus Portman were stopped, before he took on big-hitting Mancunian Matthew Hall on his own patch at the MEN Arena. Hall decked him three times and ended the Pryce reign in two.

Bradley's extra-curricular indiscretions and the resultant visa difficulties meant he missed out on a Las Vegas fight on the Joe Calzaghe-Bernard Hopkins undercard and when Joe retired later that year, father Enzo took a backward step as well. Pryce spent time with Gary Lockett and then Jamie Arthur, before becoming self-managed as his career headed into the closing chapters.

There were still some decent successes – twice over Michael Lomax, as well as against Danny Butler and Patrick Mendy – but he found himself mostly on the receiving end. Unbeaten Belarussian Sergey Rabchenko outclassed him in Bulgaria with the European light-middle belt at stake, while others on the way up also added his name to their CVs: Chris Eubank, Jr, Sam Sheedy, Frankie Gavin and Rick Skelton beat him in Britain, while Dane Torben Keller and Pole Damian Jonak did so before their own folk.

Pryce was invited to Dublin to contest the Boxing Union of Ireland's Celtic Warrior belt at middleweight against local hero Luke Keeler. When Keeler failed the scales, the flexible BUI promptly adjusted the title to super-middle. Referee Mickey Vann, handling the last contest of his illustrious career, signed off by giving the local a clear decision and left Pryce vowing to drop back in weight.

But the lure of the lucre persuaded him to take a short-notice trip to Preston to face unbeaten Zach Parker, again at super-middle. Bradley, complaining of eye problems, was halted in four and announced he would end a fine career.

Boxing is a tenacious mistress, however, and he was back four months later losing on points to unbeaten Scot Kieran Smith. Even a stoppage loss to unbeaten prospect Scott Fitzgerald, a former Commonwealth gold medallist, has not convinced Pryce to hang up the gloves. So, for the moment, the saga continues.

Still ready for action - Brad shows no sign of retirement

GAVIN REES
(1980-)

- WBA Light-Welterweight Champion 2007-08

- WBC Lightweight Challenger 2013

- European Lightweight Champion 2011-12

- British Lightweight Champion 2010-11, 2012

- WBO Inter-Continental Featherweight Champion 2001

The Welshman's world title challenge may have been on home soil, but he was not supposed to win. For even though he was facing a French champion, Souleymane M'Baye was the promoter's man.

Frank Warren had signed up the WBA's top-ranked light-welterweight with the openly expressed desire that M'Baye should whip Ricky Hatton, following the Mancunian's acrimonious split with the Sports Network organisation. The pair never met, but M'Baye had nevertheless won the vacant WBA belt and was due another fight. Warren also managed Gavin Rees, who boasted a 26-fight unbeaten record, so why not put the Newbridge

Gavin Rees

man in with his French ace? The two eventually came face to face at Cardiff International Arena on July 21, 2007.

There was a vast difference in experience: Souleymane's solitary defeat had been on points against then-WBA boss Vivian Harris, while he had beaten former holder Khalid Rahilou, Raul Balbi and Andriy Kotelnik. Rees's opposition came largely from the journeyman class.

Gavin had first laced on the gloves at nine, when grandfather Bill took him to the rickety old gym alongside Newbridge rugby ground. Under the tutelage of the inimitable Enzo Calzaghe, he proceeded to win four Welsh schools titles but, with his senior ambitions stymied by the split in the Welsh ABA, opted to turn pro at just 18.

At the time Rees weighed 10st, but his mentor ordered him to shed a stone. And it was at featherweight that he was to claim his first honour, halting Bulgarian substitute Vladimir Borov in four on April 4, 2001, at the CIA to acquire the WBO Inter-Continental strap. He saw off Russian challenger Nikolai Eremeev on a wide points verdict six months later around the corner at the National Ice Rink, but was never again to box in the division.

How it all started - Gavin with lifelong pal Bradley Pryce and mentor Enzo Calzaghe

In fact, for the next six years Gavin did little more than mark time, his sometimes casual attitude to training partly responsible. He was matched with American Mike Anchondo for an interim WBO super-feather belt, but failed the Board's check-weigh a fortnight before and had to withdraw. After missing the whole of 2005 through suspension following a spot of bother after a funeral, Rees was booked for a WBU lightweight clash with Scot Martin Watson only for a hand injury to scupper that; when the pair were rematched for the Celtic title, Gavin failed the scales.

Despite his 100 per cent record it was something of a surprise when Warren came up with the crack at M'Baye, who was also six inches taller than the Welshman. Few pundits gave him a chance. Yet Rees turned in the performance of a lifetime to upset the odds – he was 7-1 against – and to do so comfortably.

M'Baye seemed to take victory for granted, even as the home fighter claimed the early sessions. There was a heavy right in the third which made Gavin hold briefly, but otherwise Souleymane, never able to match the challenger's workrate, rarely threatened. Either the Parisian did not realise his crown was slipping or he was simply unable to react to the situation. At the final bell, margins of four, five and eight points underlined the stocky valley boy's right to call himself a world champion.

Eight months later the title had gone. Rees was back at the CIA on March 22, 2008, to face Kotelnik, a match insisted on by the WBA when they sanctioned Rees's title shot. The Hamburg-based Ukrainian was installed as favourite, no doubt influenced by Gavin's revelation that his weight-making system involved a 24-hour fast followed by a visit to McDonald's. Unsurprisingly, he was over the limit at the first attempt.

"I'm going to be a world champion" - Gavin celebrates in the closing seconds against M'Baye

Kotelnik, a former Olympic silver medallist, needed a couple of rounds to settle, but from then it was pretty much one-way traffic. He blocked most of Rees's shots, particularly to the body, while spearing in accurate punches to the Welshman's head, especially on the too-frequent occasions that Gavin let his hands drop. By the midway stage the champion was already feeling the pace, marking up below the left eye and shipping some solid left hooks to end the seventh.

By the 11th, the Newbridge boy was blowing hard, bleeding from the nose and struggling to keep his tormentor at bay. A left hook rocked him early in the last and a right scrambled his senses, so that he slipped to the canvas when Andriy broke away from a clinch. Referee Luis Pabón helped him up and waved him back in, but the next onslaught had him reeling and this time the Puerto Rican official called a halt. Just 26 seconds remained, but survival would have made no difference: all three judges had Kotelnik comfortably ahead.

Rees stepped away from the ring for more than a year, during which time Warren ended their relationship, before bouncing back with victory in one of Matchroom's all-in-a-night Prizefighter tournaments. Coach Calzaghe was opposed to the idea, but Gavin emerged with the prize from arguably the strongest field the competition ever saw. Three-round points wins over Ted Bami, Jason Cook and Colin Lynes, all ex-European champions, saw him leave Olympia with a £32,000 cheque and renewed self-belief.

With son Joe retired, little Enzo had lost much of his enthusiasm for the sport and Rees linked up with former

Just eight months later, Rees loses the crown to Kotelnik

stablemate Gary Lockett, now a rising trainer himself. A drop to lightweight saw him matched with unbeaten Scouser John Watson for the vacant British title in his new class. They met at the Newport Centre on November 6, 2010.

Again Rees was conceding substantial height and reach, but still managed to outbox him in the first half of the contest – Gavin credited this ability to two decades of sparring beanpole best friend Bradley Pryce – while the inexperienced Watson struggled to get into the fight. The local seemed to lose his way in the middle rounds, the Liverpudlian hurting him in the seventh, but the 10th saw Rees unleash a right which decked Watson, the bell preventing a follow-up. It was a brief reprieve. A thumping left brought referee Victor Loughlin's intervention midway through the 11th.

The mid-bout slump had been a worry, however, and it recurred when Gavin faced undefeated Irishman Andrew Murray for the vacant European belt at the CIA – now called the Motorpoint Arena – on June 4, 2011. The lanky Murray could hardly lay a glove on the busy Welshman for seven rounds. Then Rees blew up and had to draw deeply on his mental resources to rally in the closing exchanges and secure a clear unanimous verdict.

When first challenger Derry Mathews visited Newport four months later, a fourth-round clash of heads left Mathews with a broken nose and a Technical Draw in the records. But Gavin came through the exam next time out, outclassing former holder Anthony Mezaache in his native Clichy and finishing him in the seventh, just the stage in fights when Rees had been finding things hard.

Gavin goes down bravely to the outstanding (and obnoxious) Broner

Next up was a rematch with Mathews, this time in Sheffield. 'Dirty Derry', as he ironically called himself, had picked up Gavin's old Lonsdale Belt while waiting, so both titles were on the line. When a coming together left Mathews bleeding from the left eye in the third, there were fears of another anti-climax, but the cut was insignificant and Rees's strength proved decisive in forcing an ninth-round stoppage.

Suddenly the Newbridge warrior's name was being mentioned in the US and he was offered a shot at the "new Mayweather", Floyd's equally brash protégé, Adrien Broner, who had moved from super-feather to win the WBC lightweight strap in his previous outing. Rees would be his first challenger, on February 16, 2013, at Atlantic City's Boardwalk Hall, venue of trainer Lockett's own world title tilt at Kelly Pavlik. In both cases, the Welsh visitor was a long-odds underdog.

Not that it seemed to bother Gavin. After holding his own in the pre-fight mind games, Rees showed no fear when the bell rang, taking the action to the champion and raising a few eyebrows in an apathetic crowd who had expected a walkover. When he responded to a Broner bolo in the second round with a thumping left hook as the American lowered his hands, there were a few cheers for the visitor.

But Broner's reputation was not entirely hype. He had speed, power and a wide variety of punches; by the end of the third they were getting through. The next round saw a right uppercut drop Gavin and although he survived the round, the writing was on the wall.

Girlfriend Kayleigh left ringside. Lockett, while assuring referee Earl Brown that his pupil could continue, privately warned Gavin that he was taking too much, but the courageous challenger went to meet his fate. He even clowned for a while, but a body shot floored him again and when Broner forced him to the ropes, it was time for Lockett to mount the ring apron and wave the towel to end it.

Many thought that would be that. But four months later Rees was in the Bolton Arena, facing Anthony Crolla for the vacant WBO Inter-Continental strap, with the ceaseless chanting of the Crolla fans perhaps influencing a disputed majority verdict. Gavin, disillusioned, pondered retirement, but instead found himself involved in arguably the best contest of his career, a British title eliminator against long-time friend Gary Buckland in front of 4,000 enthralled fans at the Motorpoint Arena.

In a titanic tussle, Gavin scored to the body, often driving the Cardiff man backwards; Buckland used his reach to land hooks and jabs, marking up his rival's face. Each time a fighter looked to be fading, he discovered some new energy and stormed back into the fray. At the end of a ferocious last frame, it seemed Rees had done enough. Judge Ian John-Lewis agreed, but his two colleagues favoured Buckland.

A rematch was inevitable. Rees, who had acquired 'Rock's Bar' in Newbridge – setting up a gym at the back, where he now runs Pantside ABC – and was planning marriage to Kayleigh, announced it would be his last hurrah and was determined not to go out on a run of losses. Gary, who could have been forgiven for sidestepping his old mate, agreed to another 12-rounder at the same venue, even though this time there was no official label on the bout.

This time Gavin used his superior boxing skills to avoid trouble and, for all Buckland's best efforts, was always in control. Somehow Richie Davies had the local boy three points ahead at the end, but the other judges had margins of four and five points in favour of Rees.

All over - Gavin with twin daughters Abigail and Michaela after his final fight

Inevitably, there were calls for him to carry on, but coach Lockett revealed the pair had talked about that beforehand. "'If I look really good,' Gavin told me, 'promise me not to train me again.' So I promised," said Gary. "He was having trouble with his hands, his elbows and everything. He had a fantastic career and it was a great way to finish."

ROBBIE REGAN
(1968-)

🔥 **WBO Bantamweight Champion 1996-1998**

🔥 **IBF Interim Flyweight Champion 1995**

🔥 **British Flyweight Champion 1991, 1991-1992**

🔥 **European Flyweight Champion 1992-1993, 1994-1995**

🔥 **Welsh Flyweight Champion 1991**

It should have been a night of celebration at Cardiff International Arena. Two Welsh boxers were to enter the ring as world champions, each due to make the first defence of his hard-won crown. But while Joe Calzaghe blew away Branco Sobot to set the pattern for a decade of undisturbed dominance, Robbie Regan climbed between the ropes to announce that he would fight no more.

Robbie Regan

Winning a world title should be the key to global acclaim and financial security, but it had not turned out that way for the little man from Bargoed. Instead, victory over Puerto Rican Daniel Jiménez had been followed by nearly two years of illness and frustration.

Repeated bouts of kidney disease had forced the cancellation of scheduled defences against Scot Drew Docherty and mandatory challenger Jorge Eliécer Julio. Finally, it seemed the malady had been overcome. Julio, having won an interim belt as the WBO, with commendable patience, waited for Regan to recover, arrived in Wales for the long awaited showdown. Then, three days before fight night, came the hammer blow.

Manager Dai Gardiner was leaving the venue following the traditional head-to-head press conference when his phone rang. There was a problem. Robbie's brain scan had revealed an anomaly. The Board could not license him.

Promoter Frank Warren, angry that the routine medical had been left so late, nevertheless arranged for the Welshman to travel to London and undergo further tests. The results were the same. Not merely his reign as world champion, but his whole career was over. No wonder there were tears.

Such a hammer blow would have destroyed many men. It was not easy for Regan, who resorted to drink, resulting in brushes with the law and a spell behind bars. Thankfully, recent years have seen him defy his demons and he has been fêted at functions as far afield as Monte Carlo and Thailand, while passing on his ring wisdom to kids at Cefn Fforest.

It had been a long road. Enthused by watching boxing on TV, the 15-year-old Regan headed for the Fleur-de-Lys gym, where trainer Gardiner was making a tentative return to the sport after a three-year break following the tragic death of his pupil, Johnny Owen. Watched over by his uncle, Pat Chidgey, Robbie soon convinced Gardiner that he might be the one to conquer the peak which Owen had lost his life trying to scale.

Junior success was followed by three Welsh senior titles and a trip to the Commonwealth Games before he turned pro at 20 and drew his debut against Swansea's Eric George, who had controversially outscored him in a fourth Welsh ABA final. His first victory came with a six-round decision over Londoner Francis Ampofo, despite Regan having been on the lash at his brother's wedding.

Robbie's seventh fight brought him his first title, outpointing Garnant's Kevin Jenkins for the vacant Welsh fly belt at Cardiff's National Sports Centre on February 12, 1991, flooring the Amman Valley man in the seventh. The new champion's post-fight priority was to get the autographs of TV pundits and world title challengers Colin Jones and Jim McDonnell – not realising that he would surpass the achievements of both.

With British champion Pat Clinton having vacated, the Board nominated Regan to face one of Pat's victims, fellow Scot Joe Kelly, to decide his successor. Manager Gardiner and promotional ally Kevin Hayde tempted Kelly to Sophia Gardens on May 28, 1991, and, despite badly blistered feet, Robbie, recently made redundant from his job with a furniture company, never allowed the visitor to find any rhythm. At just 5ft, Joe kept trying to get inside, but to no avail as the Welshman took referee Dave Parris's verdict by a two-round margin. Jubilant fans proceeded to drink the bar dry.

Regan takes European title from Salvatore Fanni

First to challenge was a familiar face in Bethnal Green's Ampofo, who spent much of the time with his shaven skull in close proximity to that of the snub-nosed Regan. Inevitably, there were collisions; equally inevitably, they caused cuts. And one such gash, over his left eye, saw Robbie rescued in the penultimate round by referee Mickey Vann.

Three months later Ampofo was back in Cardiff, this time on boxing's first appearance at the National Ice Rink, fulfilling his promise of a rematch. Robbie had led when the previous bout was aborted and he duly kept the shorter Ampofo – and his hard head – at a safe distance to finish four rounds clear on John Coyle's card.

There was some hopeful talk about a crack at recently crowned IBF king Dave McAuley, but Regan was keen to have a Lonsdale Belt to keep and Ayrshire pipefitter James Drummond was invited to the Ice Rink. After an even opening, Robbie took control and the Scot's unease was reflected in frequent complaints to third man Paul Thomas. When Drummond claimed a kidney punch had decked him in the ninth, the Derby official kept counting and, although James rose at nine, matters were curtailed a few punches later.

Promoter Barry Hearn and local partner Hayde found £50,000 to bring European ruler Salvatore Fanni to Wales. The Sardinian fisherman's son seemed unfazed by the Ice Rink atmosphere and the fervent rendition of *Hen Wlad fy Nhadau* which preceded the first bell. Indeed, he started well, his two-fisted assaults accompanied by a bobbing defence which made him difficult to nail.

But by the fifth Robbie was beginning to take the measure of the smaller man, landing a series of jabs before bringing in the occasional body shot to help slow the visitor. Fanni drew on impressive stamina to close the final margins to one, two and three points, but the belt was heading for the Rhymney Valley.

Danny Porter, who had drawn with Fanni on his own soil, was bullish when he arrived at the newly rebranded Welsh Institute of Sport for their oft-postponed showdown, but the redhead from Hitchin had a lot less to say after he was dazzled and dismantled inside three rounds by an unusually aggressive Regan.

Robbie, now ranked by all the main sanctioning bodies, relinquished his European honour to seek a world title opportunity. But none of the holders wanted to visit Wales; Regan was reluctant to travel. Amid the acrimony, Frank Warren took over the promotional reins, but Robbie eventually had to retrace his steps and challenge another Italian for his old European strap. US-based Luigi Camputaro had beaten Fanni to claim the belt and faced Regan in Cardiff on November 19, 1994.

A technically intriguing contest contained several rounds difficult to score after Camputaro had taken

How Boxing News reported Robbie's defeat by Alberto Jiménez

the early lead. Robbie, again hampered by blisters after rashly boxing in new boots, battled back into contention in an absorbing scrap which had the Ice Rink faithful in such a frenzy that nobody heard the bell to end the 11th. Both were cut, while Regan was docked a point for straying low, but two of the officials favoured the home fighter and he once again ruled Europe.

This time victory did lead to the opportunity Regan craved. New WBO fly supremo Alberto Jiménez, from the Mexico City slums, accepted the financial realities and agreed to face Robbie in Cardiff, although an abscess on the knuckles of his left hand forced the challenger to seek a three-week postponement.

Before they came together at the Ice Rink on June 17, 1995, Regan needed pain-killing jabs to make his left mitt serviceable, and was soon to be further handicapped by a swollen right eye and a cut over the other. Jiménez was in charge from the start – his body barrages were particularly effective and one judge gave him each of the nine rounds the fight lasted – until cornerman Gardiner draped a towel over his man's head and told him it was over. Regan wept throughout a TV interview with Barry McGuigan and it seemed that his fistic journey might be done.

But before the end of the year Regan was to contest another belt – or so it seemed. After IBF ruler Danny Romero, scheduled to defend against unbeaten Tunisian Ferid ben Jeddou, cried off with a fractured eye socket that threatened to sideline him for months, his frustrated challenger was paired with the Welshman for the organisation's interim belt. But when the IBF's representative, Bobby Lee, Jr, turned up for the weigh-in, he insisted the bout was merely a final eliminator. Ben Jeddou, a shot at Romero already booked, threatened to pull out, while the home camp were equally irate. Warren, in Philadelphia to watch Mike Tyson, was, coincidentally, in the same hotel as IBF president Bobby Lee, Sr; a few strong words and suddenly it was for the interim title once more.

The Italy-based North African southpaw, the first lefty Regan had faced, proved no match for the Welshman, who hurt his opponent in the opening minute and battered him so severely at the end of the first that Ferid had to clutch the top rope to find his way to the corner. Halfway through the second session, a single left hook dropped Ben Jeddou on his face and referee Roy Francis called an immediate halt so that he could receive treatment.

The IBF had not brought a belt – the WBO were to prove equally remiss in due course – and Robbie was formally presented with one of their inter-continental straps, rushed down the motorway from the Salford home of its owner, Steve Foster, but the crowd at the Institute of Sport, unaware of the backstage goings-on, cheered their idol to the echo.

But when his son was safely back in New Jersey, Bobby Lee, Sr, reverted to the "final eliminator" story, claiming the weigh-in U-turn had been in order to save the show. Then, with Romero surprisingly announcing he was fit again, Lee contradicted himself and said Regan *had* been interim ruler, but one was no longer needed. Fellow-American Mark Johnson was mysteriously elevated to

Daniel Jiménez lands a left, but loses his crown

the No 1 spot and Romero was to defend against him. But the champion pronounced that he could no longer make flyweight – and the IBF agreed Robbie should now meet Johnson to decide his successor.

With the authority's stance changing almost hourly, Warren eventually gave up on them and turned his focus back to the WBO and another Jiménez, a Puerto Rican named Daniel, who had won and defended their bantam belt on Sports Network bills in London. The deal was easy to do and they came together at the Institute of Sport on April 26, 1996.

Gardiner's tactics were for Robbie to move in and out, but after three rounds it became clear that Jiménez had to be put under pressure. It proved a successful switch, Regan staying close and outworking the champion, eventually dropping him with a left hook late in the eighth.

A burst ulcer in his mouth meant the Welshman was swallowing blood for the last few sessions, with Daniel finishing on top and convinced his title was safe. But there were no doubts among the men who mattered: Dutch and Canadian judges had three points between them, their colleague from Luxembourg a generous five, all for Regan. When MC Mike Goodall uttered those magic words "and the NEW ..." Robbie burst into tears and threw himself into Gardiner's arms, while the fans' roar meant the rest of the sentence was inaudible.

Nobody could have guessed the winner would never box again. When Regan made his farewell speech at the CIA 21 months later, he thanked his loyal supporters and told them, "If you are just a little bit as proud of me as I am of all of you, I'll retire a happy man."

We *are* proud of you, Robbie. And much more than a little bit.

A tearful Regan tells the CIA crowd he will fight no more

DICK RICHARDSON
(1934-1999)

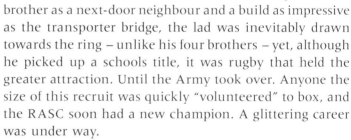

- European Heavyweight Champion 1960-1962

- Empire Heavyweight Challenger 1957, 1963

- British Heavyweight Challenger 1963

National Service had as many detractors as supporters, and when it disappeared from British life in 1962 few mourned its passing. But it turned a big, but limited young rugby player into one of the best heavyweights Wales has produced.

Driver Richardson, R.A. was sent to join the Royal Army Service Corps at Elles Barracks, Farnborough, in 1953. The PTI there was Johnny Lewis, a Welsh-speaking Cockney lightweight with parents from Aberaeron, who was managed by Wally Lesley. And Lesley's shrewd guidance was to help provide the one-time plasterer from Newport with a comfortable existence.

Dick, brought up in the Maesglas area of the town, inherited courage from his father, who had been a wall of death rider. With Johnny Basham's

brother as a next-door neighbour and a build as impressive as the transporter bridge, the lad was inevitably drawn towards the ring – unlike his four brothers – yet, although he picked up a schools title, it was rugby that held the greater attraction. Until the Army took over. Anyone the size of this recruit was quickly "volunteered" to box, and the RASC soon had a new champion. A glittering career was under way.

In 1954 he won the Army heavyweight title and on demob took up an invitation to call on Lesley, wearing a Teddy Boy suit with jacket nearly touching the ground, and trousers as narrow as chairlegs. Deciding that he shouldn't allow Dick's sartorial eccentricities to stand in his way, the former market porter from the Elephant and Castle agreed to take him on. It was a decision neither regretted.

Dick Richardson

Wally found the Welshman a job delivering milk – where

he could keep an eye on him each morning – and introduced him to the pro game at Harringay against Jim Cooper, a lad he'd flattened as an amateur. He dropped the Londoner twice in the first, but Cooper recovered to take the decision – and twin brother Henry made a winning pro debut on the same bill. But there was only one defeat in Dick's next 19 fights, and that was via disqualification.

He had also built quite a following, as demonstrated when he met the German, Robert Warmbrunn, at Abergavenny's Market Hall. There were mile-long traffic jams, followed by pandemonium as fans tried to gain entry in time for the main event. They stormed the gates, clambered over barriers and partitions, even used the window of the ladies' lavatory to get in. And all for a massacre that lasted just 105 seconds!

An all-Welsh showdown with Joe Erskine at Maindy Stadium, an eliminator in all but name, proved a barn-burner. Richardson cut his Cardiff rival early on and dropped him in the fifth, but lost the verdict at the end of 10 pulsating rounds.

Joe went on to win the British crown, while Dick concentrated on picking up regular pay cheques against a series of imports. It took promoter Jack Solomons 11 transatlantic phone calls and five cables to get the services of former world champion Ezzard Charles, but he must have wondered whether it was worth the trouble. The American showed little desire to entertain, repeatedly holding until referee Frank Wilson turfed him out in the second.

The next visitor to cross the Pond was more combative. Big Cuban Niño Valdés had already destroyed Don Cockell in two and lapped it up when Dick foolishly went in brawling. A left hook felled the Welshman in the second, and by the end of the eighth, Richardson's right eye had swollen like a black plum and referee Andrew Smyth heeded Lesley's suggestion that he stop it.

Former British champion Johnny Williams was hired to graft some skill on to Dick's natural strength, but there were still a lot of rough edges when he tried for his first title, against Empire king Joe Bygraves at Maindy Stadium on May 27, 1957. Bygraves, 26 the day before the fight, was at his peak, having recently knocked out Henry Cooper.

Richardson and Joe Bygraves battle to a draw

This time the Jamaican had all the trouble he could handle, in a contest that the Marquis of Queensberry might have had difficulty recognising. Both were soon in trouble for illegal headwork and after-the-bell exchanges, but the fans loved it. The pair were rocked in turn, blood flowing from both, but at the end of 15 torrid sessions referee Eugene Henderson was unable to part them on his scorecard. Bygraves had kept his title.

Willie Pastrano and Bob Baker underlined Richardson's limitations with points wins, while the Gwent fighter's billy-goat tendencies saw him disqualified against another rated American, Cleveland Williams. A rematch was arranged for Coney Beach, prompting an episode as bizarre as any in the colourful history of the sport.

First the visitor refused to weigh in at the venue because it lacked central heating – in July! Next he claimed illness, but four doctors found nothing wrong. Finally, Cleveland's acting manager, Bill Gore, confessed. "My boy has had a message from beyond," he told the incredulous Pressmen. "Call it hoodoo or voodoo, he thought it would be bad for him to fight tonight." And the Yanks headed for home.

It was different when 'Our 'Enery' visited Porthcawl. The bout was even enough until the fifth, when Dick felled the already bleeding Cooper with a clubbing right-left combination. Charging in to end matters, Richardson ran into a whirlwind. A left to the side made him gasp, another left landed flush on his open mouth and a right spreadeagled him over the ropes. Eyes blurred, he took an eight count, but Henry efficiently pounded him until referee Ike Powell leapt between them. Dick slid to the canvas, there to be attended by his grieving cornermen amid the silence of a stunned arena.

Erskine easily outscored him before 12,000 soaking supporters at Coney Beach, but the Newportonian was soon to pick up an unexpected title, accepting a late call to Germany to tackle former victim Hans Kalbfell for the vacant European belt. There were 15,000 at the Westfalenhalle in Dortmund on March 27, 1960, as Richardson, after a decent start, began to fall behind. The German, however, tired and late in the 13th he was dropped by a right hook; as soon as he got up, seconds before the bell, Dick, without waiting for the referee's go-ahead, brought over another right which laid Hans out at his feet.

Photographers flooded the ring, snapping away over the unconscious German in the thought that he had won on a disqualification; French official Robert Vaisberg then lifted Richardson's arm, and bedlam broke out. Dick needed a police escort to the dressing-room, and the arguments continued through the night. The British team said Mr Vaisberg's pre-fight homily had included the information that there would be no "Box on" – if a man was vertical, you could hit him. The ref himself claimed he had stopped

German police provide an escort as cornerman Frank Duffett leads Dick to safety following his controversial win over Kalbfell

the contest as Kalbfell rose; the fight was therefore over before the alleged illegal punch was thrown.

But the post-fight scenes were nothing compared with what would follow at Porthcawl when Richardson risked his title against the 'Blackpool Bomber', Brian London. The more skilful London treated Dick with scorn, sticking his ample chin out in invitation and irritatingly extending his left glove beneath the champion's nose. Anger was never far below the surface and Brian, already bleeding from the left eye, recoiled from a seventh-round clash claiming a butt.

The start of the eighth saw London charge across the ring and referee Andy Smyth had to restrain him from attacking the Welshman while he was still on his stool. At the end of the session the referee went to Brian's corner, and, after agitated exchanges with his seconds, emerged to announce the challenger's retirement. But if Brian had had enough, his family were certainly keen to continue. Father Jack, himself an ex-champion, and Jack, Jr, also a former pro, hurled themselves at Dick and his handlers, and it needed the police to restore order.

More trouble might have been expected when Richardson returned to Dortmund for another meeting with the bitter Kalbfell, and the Welshman was jeered all the way from his dressing-room. But Dick clearly had the better of a bruising battle and the generous Germans cheered him all the way back.

A year later the Welshman went back again to Dortmund to take on the new German hope, 23-year-old Karl Mildenberger. It was the first time Dick had met a southpaw and he was well prepared. Before the fight Lesley

Richardson has treatment after being knocked out by Ingemar Johansson

said, "We've told him to move to his right and throw his own right." After two minutes and 25 seconds of the first, Dick did just that. Ten seconds later, Mildenberger had been counted out. "I was going to follow up with my left," said Dick, "but he was already on the canvas."

Ingemar Johansson, however, was a different matter. His world crown reclaimed by former holder Floyd Patterson, he returned to Europe seeking his old throne. And on June 17, 1962, in the Ullevi Stadium, Gothenburg, where a Pelé goal four years earlier had ousted Wales from the World Cup, Richardson, too, was knocked out, for the first time in his career. The 'Hammer of Thor', as the Swede called his right hand, left Dick under the bottom rope with 47 seconds left of the eighth. Johansson departed for his postponed honeymoon; Richardson headed home an ex-champion.

There was one more shot in his locker. Cooper had been ordered to defend his British and Empire titles against the Newport man, and they met at Wembley on March 26, 1963. The cut-prone Londoner bled from the opener, with Dick disrupting his rhythm. But in the closing stages of the fifth, Henry followed a jab with three superb left hooks to the head. A body shot brought the Welshman's hands down and an inch-perfect left landed on his jaw with all the finality of an executioner's axe.

Two knockouts in successive contests spelt a message as clear as any received by Cleveland Williams, and five days after the Cooper fight the man they called the 'Maesglas Marciano' announced his retirement. But his life still had its share of blood and guts – he ran a butcher's shop at Frimley Green, the Surrey town where he was married, and where he died in 1999.

Henry Cooper waits for the referee to complete his count and put an end to Richardson's career

JIMMY ROBERTS
(1926-1981)

Welsh Middleweight Champion 1952

Boxers didn't waste time back in the day. The Newbridge southpaw's whole pro career was crammed into little over a year, but he still managed to win and lose the Welsh middleweight crown.

Jimmy Roberts began with a lively draw with Tredegar's Eddie Williams on a Tommy Farr undercard at Cardiff Arms Park and there was another draw at Abergavenny's Market Hall against Coldstream Guards sergeant Don Roberts, but six victories established Jimmy as one to watch and he was considered good enough to box an exhibition with former world champion Randy Turpin at Carmarthen.

Jimmy's first setback came against a fellow-southpaw. Former amateur star Roy Agland, from Tiryberth, had been out of the ring for 20 months, but was still able to turn on a masterclass of sheer boxing ability and, at the end of eight rounds, defeat had arrived at Jimmy's door. But when the Welsh Area Council put their heads together to consider the first challenger for newly crowned Welsh middle ruler Ron Cooper, they still plumped for Roberts.

And when Jimmy entered the ring to face Cooper on August 20, 1952, at Coney Beach Arena, he showed that the decision-makers were not too far off the mark after all, ending the Pyle man's reign after just 11 weeks. The ringwise titleholder took the first few rounds, courtesy of an accurate left lead, but Roberts had youth and strength on his side and these gradually began to tell, underlined by a left to the jaw late in the fifth which sent Cooper to the canvas for a count of eight.

It marked a turning point, with Jimmy's work inside compounding the damage. Ron's resilience was notable, particularly in a torrid last round, but the inevitable verdict sparked extra celebration in the Roberts corner as it marked a fourth reigning Welsh champion for Swansea-based manager Eddie Evans.

Jimmy Roberts

Perhaps the jubilation impaired their judgment a little. They agreed to take a late substitute job at Belle Vue in Manchester against big-hitting Bruce Crawford, a Tees-sider whose string of stoppages included his last two outings. Three rounds and three knockdowns completed his hat-trick.

With Agland awaiting his chance, new promoter Syd Evans, a local quarry owner, went for an idea that would become common in later years, showcasing both side by side at Abergavenny's Market Hall. Roberts returned to the win column by outpointing the heavier Jackie Marr, while Agland finished his task in four rounds.

Back at the same venue on December 1, 1952, the pair went at it to dispute the title. The challenger had advantages in height and reach and picked Roberts off as he tried to move in. Jimmy took the blows well and handed out his own two-fisted punishment in a bout that was still level at the halfway stage.

But the Agland power was taking its effect and the champion had little left when they emerged for the 10th round, a right hook felling him for eight. Battered around the ring, Roberts clung desperately to the ropes before subsiding to the canvas; when the count again reached eight, he tried to drag himself upright, but pitched forward, insensible.

In the absence of a stretcher, he was ferried to the dressing room on one of the press tables. Still unconscious, he was transferred to Abergavenny Cottage Hospital, where he regained his wits during the night, but was detained for 10 days. It was the end of his brief life as a boxer.

Roberts and his wife, Doreen, ran the Homestead Café in Brynmawr for more than 16 years before retiring to a Victorian cottage at Lydbrook, in the Forest of Dean. In the small hours of November 12, 1981, an articulated lorry carrying 19 tons of sheet steel crashed into the house, leaving his wife and one son, Cross Keys flanker Craig, seriously injured. Jimmy, still only 54, was killed instantly.

JEROME SAMUELS
(1993-)

🥊 Welsh Light-Middleweight Champion 2014-15

Sometimes it just needs someone who believes in you. Jerome Samuels had inherited much of father Paul's talent and had proved it by winning Welsh schools and junior titles. When he turned pro at 18, hopes were high. Then he lost his first five fights.

The debut defeat was predictable. Needing the money, the Newport youngster agreed to make his bow against unbeaten Rhondda southpaw Lewis Rees, a multiple amateur champion. Rees duly floored him four times and it was all over early in the second. Next time out, again before a hometown crowd, he was thrown in with another undefeated operator, Chris Higgs, from Lydney, but trained in Gwent by Tony Borg. Higgs won every round.

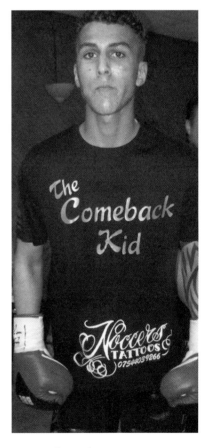

Trips to Birmingham and Barnsley brought losses to another two opponents with 100 per cent records, before debutant Rod Smith knocked him out in a round at Rotherham. It was time for a major rethink.

Samuels left manager Steve Sims to be guided by Londoner Greg Steene and trained by Richie Garner, a solicitor and former sparmate of his father. And everything changed. Their first bout together, in Southampton, involved yet another unbeaten foe, but Jerome took a clear decision. Then he won another three, two of them on home ground, where he stopped Cardiff traveller Tom Price in the first and then outpointed Blackwood trier Dai Jones. It was close enough for them to be matched again at the Newport Centre on March 14, 2014, with the vacant Welsh light-middle title at stake.

Jerome Samuels

Watched by his father, winner of the same belt 16 years earlier, the youngster's speed and accuracy of punch, aided by considerable height and reach advantages, overcame the all-action efforts of the stocky Jones. Dai's attempts to get inside meant his head was frequently in Samuels's face, with Jerome holding to avoid a collision, which made for a messy, if competitive spectacle.

But the cleaner work came from the 20-year-old and if referee Clarke Joslyn, in his first championship action, saw it closer than many with his 97-96 card, the right man had his arm raised. Yet all was not well beyond the ropes and mentor Garner walked away.

Back with Sims in the corner he defended against the naturally bigger Rhondda southpaw, Barrie Jones, in Newport on March 13, 2015. The Ferndale man, normally a slow starter, went off like a train and Jerome never came to terms with his task. The champion dropped to a knee in the third and was still under pressure when referee Reece Carter stepped in.

The loss of his title prompted another change. He extended his managerial contract with Steene and kissed and made up with coach Garner. Unfortunately, there was no immediate success, a torn bicep forcing Jerome out after three rounds against Portsmouth's unbeaten Michael McKinson. And since then there has been no sign of him. Still young, it is to be hoped that he may yet fulfil his promise.

PAUL SAMUELS
(1973-)

- Welsh Light-Middleweight Champion 1998-2001

- Interim IBF Inter-Continental Light-Middleweight Champion 1999

- British Light-Middleweight Challenger 2000

- IBO Light-Middleweight Challenger 2002

It is one of the most-watched boxing clips on YouTube. Paul Samuels, from Newport, and Peterborough lad Cello Renda circle each other awaiting the chance to pounce. Then they strike, in the same split second, each landing with a vicious left hook, sending the other flying. It was typical of one of Wales's most exciting fighters in recent years.

The youngest of seven children, he was brought up in the game: there was even a punchball in the front room of the family home on the Bettws

Double knockdown - Paul Samuels (right) and Cello Renda both hit the deck

estate. Encouraged by their father, Sierra Leone-born Jake, the three older brothers – John, Chris and Gerald – all boxed for Wales, Paul following suit in due course.

Yet the baby was the best. Five schoolboy titles were followed by another two at youth level and two more in the Welsh boys' clubs championships. Unlike some, he carried his success into the seniors, winning Welsh ABA honours at three different weights.

He was the first of the family to dip his toes into the pro ranks. Although an amateur with Crindau Harlequins in his hometown, he headed up the valley to the burgeoning Enzo Calzaghe gym at Newbridge, joining the trainer's son, Joe, under the management of Mickey Duff and Terry Lawless.

Paul followed the Calzaghes to Frank Warren and had his first shot at a belt, taking on North Walian puncher Craig Winter for the vacant Welsh light-middle throne at Bristol's Whitchurch Sports Centre, on December 5, 1998. It was a taste of thrillers to come. Winter was generally under fire until a straight right dumped a shocked Samuels on his backside. In the second, the Gwent fighter, who, despite moving up from welter, had needed two attempts to make 11st, launched a thunderous left hook and Craig collapsed on to his face, staggering up just as referee Wynford Jones reached 10.

When Paul halted 35-year-old American Eric Holland on cuts in nine rounds at Cardiff International Arena, he was crowned IBF Inter-Continental champion. Then Evans Ashira, the Danish-African later to challenge Calzaghe in the same hall, pointed out that he already filled that position. Hastily backtracking – and unwilling to forgo a sanctioning fee – the IBF announced that the bout had been for the interim title instead.

It was pretty academic, as Samuels was eyeing the British honour stripped from Ensley Bingham. He had to travel to London to face Wayne Alexander on February 19, 2000, at the Goresbrook Leisure Centre, not far from Ford's giant Dagenham car factory. Given that the unbeaten pair had both been on the canvas, a proper tear-up was forecast. Nobody was disappointed.

In what the *Boxing News* headline dubbed "The British Hagler-Hearns", Paul, three inches taller, boxed calmly in an opener which saw each suffer nicks to the face. The second, too, went the Welshman's way, with Alexander switching desperately to southpaw and back. In the third the Croydon warrior hurt Samuels to the body and began to hurl bombs in a win-or-bust attack. Wayne trapped his rival on the ropes and followed two solid lefts with a series of right hooks which brought referee Paul Thomas to the rescue as Samuels fell through the ropes.

He climbed back into the ring, waving to reassure his tearful mother and girlfriend that he was OK, but his 100 per cent record had gone. In addition, it was a first loss for mentor Enzo in 63 stints in the corners of his various pupils. Samuels, feeling that the Sardinian tried to make all his charges box like son Joe, sought an alternative.

He had a period with Dai Gardiner and then Tony Borg – and, promotionally, Barry Hearn – but there was little obvious change to Paul's style when he took on former Commonwealth king Richard Williams for the IBO strap at Brentwood on June 29, 2002.

Samuels was on top when the contest came to an abrupt end in the third with Richard bleeding from two deep gashes over his right eye. Referee Richie Davies considered a head clash had been responsible – although the tape seems to back Paul's assertion that they were caused

Paul and son Jerome celebrating the youngster's first Welsh vest

by his punches – so, instead of a stoppage win, the Welshman had to settle for a Technical Draw. A rematch was inevitable and this time there were no cuts to interfere. Both enjoyed periods of ascendancy, but Williams rendered the scorecards academic in the 10th with an explosive right to the jaw. Samuels scrambled to his feet, but referee John Coyle rightly called a halt.

Paul disappeared from the scene for three years before returning to the gym to train talented, but reluctant nephew Jason. It prompted a comeback which lasted another six years, with more laments than celebrations. Future world champion Darren Barker knocked him out in one round – though Samuels had grounds for complaint, as the terminal blow came after referee had called a halt to give a count to the Londoner, whose gloves had touched the canvas following a punch by the Welshman.

Another world titleholder-in-waiting, George Groves, also won inside three minutes, as did serial challenger Paul Smith, before a fifth-round loss to Midlander Ryan Aston brought the end, one day after son Jerome had made his pro debut.

STEVE SIMS
(1958-)

- British Featherweight Champion 1982-1983

- European Featherweight Challenger 1983

- Welsh Super-Featherweight Champion 1985-86

When Barry McGuigan marked his pro debut by stopping one of the game's regular losers it was greeted, according to one writer, with euphoria hardly justified by someone becoming the 43rd fighter to beat Selvin Bell. Steve Sims also made his bow with a win over Bell: his victory was met with total apathy.

Unlike the charismatic Irishman, already laden with amateur honours, Steve was virtually unknown even in Newport. While the Clones Cyclone was tipped from the start as a future world champion, 'Sammy', as he had been called from childhood, was a novice with no greater ambition than to earn a few bob.

Steve never entered a fight gym before he was 16, and then only to improve his hand speed for kung fu, in which he was a junior black belt. Even the martial art was his second sporting choice. As a young weightlifter, Sims had been called up for the Welsh Commonwealth Games squad, but he realised that a permanently bent left arm, the legacy of an accident as a five-year-old, would not be regarded as benevolently by international judges as by those at home. He gave the squad sessions a miss, and never lifted again.

Steve Sims parades the Lonsdale Belt

Braving parental disapproval, Steve began competitive boxing at 17, but after just 19 amateur contests the coincidence of redundancy from Llanwern steelworks and impending marriage to Gaynor drove him into the pro ranks in June 1979. He had a lot to learn. The initial victory over Bell was followed by a switchback ride of wins and losses and a somewhat podgy lightweight decided to step down to feather.

'Sammy' lost seven and a half pounds in three weeks before going in with the unbeaten Clyde Ruan at Burslem. Ruan edged a disputed half-point victory, but Sims thought he won – and it was a turning point psychologically. For the first time Steve believed boxing could bring him more than just some folding money. His new-found self-confidence was not immediately shared by others and there were doubts when he was matched with former Commonwealth Games gold medallist Davy Larmour, in Belfast. Sims comprehensively outpointed him.

Steve signs for his British title shot, watched by matchmaker Les Roberts (left) and manager Billy May

Even defeats to Swansea's Don George and future bantam king John Feeney taught Sims a lot, as did regular sparring with Johnny Owen, and a draw with Devonport printer Vernon Penprase earned a rematch with British eliminator status at Newport's Ebbw Bridge Club. It proved the most gruelling evening of Steve's career, but this time referee Jim Brimmell found a winner: Sims, whose workrate, not for the last time, brought him the decision over a more skilful opponent.

Fight traders in London, still unaware of his improvement, gave Steve little chance in the final eliminator against Southern Area champion Jimmy Flint at the Albert Hall. But a new job humping hods for a pair of bricklayers had added strength, which proved invaluable in the second round, when the Wapping puncher landed enough whopping punches to crush anyone less fit. Flint seemed to believe he was invulnerable, at least against someone who had won only half his 16 pro bouts, and midway through the fourth he dropped his hands as if inviting 'Sammy' to have a go. The invitation was accepted with alacrity, two rights and a left to the jaw sending Jimmy crashing to the canvas, where he remained motionless throughout the count. Flint never boxed again; Sims himself was in a state of semi-shock.

Steve had to wait nine months for his title chance. Pat Cowdell had relinquished the crown and Steve instead took on Scot Terry McKeown at the St Andrew's Sporting Club in Glasgow on September 20, 1982. There were pre-fight problems with the Welshman's weight; it needed repeated visits to the sauna before he satisfied the scales at the second attempt.

Tactically, the Sims camp also slipped up. They expected McKeown, having seen what happened to Flint, to keep on the move and they prepared accordingly, but Terry went straight in without a backward step and his sharp punching established an early lead. 'Sammy' kept in contention, but found it difficult to make any impact. The Scot's positive tactics, however, sapped his resources and from the eighth the balance of power began to shift.

McKeown, although only five months older, tired dramatically, with Steve's body shots playing their part. In the 12th he had no resistance when Sims walked through his by now flimsy punches and clubbed home a big right hand. A follow-up onslaught drove him head-first through the ropes, and although he pulled himself back and took the count on one knee, his eyes were glazed and his will was broken. Referee Dakin continued to 10, and the redundant steelworker who turned to boxing for a few quid was the champion of Britain.

Money was still a driving force, however, and Steve was never to defend his new crown. "We were offered just £5,000 to go over to Ireland and face McGuigan," he points out. "And then I was nominated to fight for the vacant European title, and the Italians paid me £12,000 to take on Loris Stecca."

Financially, the visit to Sardinia on April 7, 1983 was no doubt more rewarding; fistically, it was no easier. The unbeaten Stecca, just turned 23, would in due course beat McGuigan to a world title, becoming the WBA king at super-bantamweight. Steve was as fit as he had ever been, but needed a painkilling jab in his right hand, and then found his stamina undermined by a moment's self-indulgence.

"I'd had to starve myself to get down to 9st," he remembers, "and the day before the fight I had a few spoonfuls of honey. I felt that guilty I took

Two Newport icons – Steve Sims on a training run up the steps of the famous Transporter Bridge

half a laxative. The next day I weighed in half a pound inside the limit, and felt great, so I had a full meal – spaghetti bolognese, roast potatoes, beef, vegetables and plenty of ice cream. I felt fine, and even went to sleep. But in the changing-room before the fight, the laxative worked and I spent threequarters of an hour on the toilet. It took all the strength out of me."

Despite the pre-fight upset, Sims moved forward throughout, only for the classy Italian to pick him off. The Welshman landed a couple in the fifth, but he was bleeding badly near the right eye and unable to see on one side. At the bell, the ringside doctor called a halt.

A week later McGuigan destroyed Vernon Penprase to claim Steve's cast-off British title and Barry's manager, Barney Eastwood, travelled to Cardiff to check out the obvious first challenger. But Sims could never cope with a six-foot Canadian southpaw, Nedrie Simmons, and any meeting with the 'Clones Cyclone' went out of the window.

A good purse compensated for the loss of two teeth against future world champion Lester Ellis in Australia – and missing the birth of daughter Danielle while he was away – but an undertrained Sims was then crushed in two rounds by Merseysider Kevin Pritchard, another who went on to win a title.

It took a new trainer, former Navy PTI Nick Newell, to revive Steve's flagging career. Victory over Porthcawl's Steve Cleak at the brand-new Newport Centre saw Sims become the first Welsh champion in the newly recognised 9st 4lb division. There was a successful defence against 21-year-old Cardiffian Tony Borg before Steve – having left Billy May for a new manager, Mac Williams – had a last crack at the big time.

It was a disaster. Sims had not made 9st for more than three years and the effort left him in no state to deal with Robert Dickie, from Cross Hands, who had won the British title by outpointing Steve's old rival, Feeney. It was his first defence, at the Ebbw Vale Leisure Centre on July 30, 1986, and the 22-year-old champion soon began ripping uppercuts through the older man's peekaboo guard. With just two seconds remaining of the fifth, Dickie dug a vicious left deep into Steve's side.

The Newport man slumped to his knees, his forehead resting on the canvas as ref John Coyle continued the count into the interval. Looking despairingly towards his corner, he struggled to force himself upright, but was unable to persuade the air into his burning lungs. It was a full minute before he could be helped to his feet.

There was not much left. African-born Dane Racheed Lawal, destined for European honours, outpointed Sims in Copenhagen, and a future world champion brought down the final curtain. After five rounds of pressure from up-and-coming Liverpudlian Paul Hodkinson, Steve, again weight-drained, subsided gently to one knee and took the count. No longer could he face the tyranny of the scales as well as ambitious young opponents; a career that had achieved more than he ever dreamed of was finally over.

But the game he entered merely to sharpen up his kung fu now has a firm hold on Steve. As a manager, trainer, promoter and matchmaker, he is still playing a key role in keeping the sport alive in his home town.

Heddwyn Taylor proudly presents

THE BRITISH FEATHERWEIGHT BOXING CHAMPIONSHIP

12 × 3 Minute Rounds at 9st.

 V

Robert Dickie   Steve Sims

on
Wednesday July 29th 1986
at
The Ebbw Vale Leisure Centre

Doors Open 7.00 p.m.
Boxing Commences at 8.00 p.m. prompt
Licenced Bars

— Sponsored by South Wales Windows —

The last hurrah - Sims came up short against Robert Dickie

KELVIN SMART
(1960-)

- British Flyweight Champion 1982-84

- Welsh Featherweight Challenger 1986

When you achieve a life's ambition and win a Lonsdale Belt, you are entitled to bask in the acclaim of the crowd. When Llanbradach's Kelvin Smart became British flyweight champion he did so in front of a few thousand still searching for their seats at Wembley Arena.

Instead of taking place in a packed Welsh hall, his clash with Swansea boy Dave George for the long-vacant throne was merely the show-opener at Wembley Arena on September 14, 1982, Smart's manager, Mickey Duff, having outbid Welsh promoter Heddwyn Taylor to stage the fight on a Colin Jones undercard.

Kelvin Smart

But you have to play the hand you are dealt. The Rhymney Valley boy did his job, forcing the pace from the start and nullifying George's normally effective jab. By the fourth Kelvin was working to the body and Dave dropped to the canvas a round later, his tormentor receiving a warning from referee Sid Nathan for hurling a punch as he rose.

Lefts to head and torso drove George back at the start of the sixth and a follow-up onslaught culminated in another left downstairs which left him with no chance of beating the count.

It was a success tipped for Smart from an early age. His schoolboy successes saw his picture featured on the cover of a new Welsh sports magazine, heralding a future star . After winning the Welsh ABA title in 1979, the blond bomber turned pro, originally with Cardiffian Benny Jacobs, and began to rack up the wins.

Only a surprise draw with former victim Mohammed Younis marred his early record, but Kelvin was to suffer a setback when he ventured to Spain to face tiny southpaw Enrique Rodríguez Cal, a former

Olympic bronze medallist, in a final eliminator for the European title held by Londoner Charlie Magri. Kicked and spat on as he walked to the Oviedo ring, Smart produced a grandstand finish, but the judges favoured the local.

For Rodríguez Cal, stopped in two by Magri, it was a last taste of victory. But Smart rebounded with the triumph over George which gave him Magri's cast-off British crown. Yet it was more than a year before the new champion boxed again, seeing off Filipino former world title

Young Kelvin with a trophy almost as big as him, watched by future manager Benny Jacobs and the great Joe Erskine

challenger Tito Abella and Angelo Dundee-trained Canadian Ian Clyde before a first defence against another Olympic bronze medallist, Hugh Russell, at Belfast's King's Hall on January 25, 1984.

Smart on the attack against Canadian Olympian Ian Clyde

The red-haired Ulsterman had already ruled briefly at bantam, but had dropped to his natural division, though even his bookie manager, Barney Eastwood, was offering 3-1 against his charge. Those that took those odds were celebrating at the end. The first six rounds were evenly divided, but the seventh saw the Irish southpaw take control, with Kelvin hampered by a swollen eye. At the bell he complained that he could not see, cornerman Duff promptly signalling his surrender.

A second-round knockout by Holyhead lifeboatman's son Ivor Jones prompted a year out, but

Kelvin in more recent times

Smart returned with a rough-house win over Midlander Rocky Lawlor. It was to be his last. Disqualification for a low blow against unbeaten Dave McAuley was followed by a draw in Scotland with local Joe Kelly, before Kelvin began to chase the cheques, travelling three times to France and once as far as Guyana.

Dai Gardiner was now holding the reins and even he had misgivings when Smart took on Peter Harris for the vacant Welsh feather title at Swansea's Patti Pavilion on November 18, 1986. They were not misplaced. Harris took a leaf out of his opponent's book and worked the body throughout, with Kelvin managing only a share of one round on referee Adrian Morgan's card.

French bantam Fabrice Benichou – like McAuley and points conqueror Thierry Jacob, a future world champion – despatched him inside a round and when St Albans prospect Sean Murphy flattened him in three it marked the end of the road for the one-time 'Mighty Atom'.

FRANK TAYLOR
(1915-2002)

⬥ Empire Games Silver Medallist 1934

The lad from Risca should not have been competing at Wembley; after all, he had lost in a box-off for selection. Indeed, if one Welsh gym instructor had had his way, he might never have become a boxer at all.

His father took 14-year-old Frank to a local club to learn the sport, only to be told that nobody under 16 could join. But young Taylor continued to turn up, making such a nuisance of himself that the trainer, hoping to get shot of him for good, invited him to try out with one of the gym stars. Frank proceeded to flatten the bigger man with a body shot – and suddenly his age was no longer a problem.

Success was far from instant. He lost in the semi-finals of the Welsh youth championships in 1932 - an event which made history in having a woman medical officer for the first time, Newport GP Sylvia Smith - but victory in a novices' competition at Cardiff's Roath Park set him on his way. Back then Taylor scaled a mere 8st 6lb, but he soon filled out, work as a collier putting muscle on a slender frame.

A wrist injury sidelined him for a while, but Frank wore the vest of Risca ABC in the 1934 Welsh ABAs and won twice before being outpointed by former Olympian Fred Perry in the lightweight semi-final. The veteran Cardiffian then lost to Newport's Phil Grace, but neither was available for the Empire Games and a box-off was arranged between Taylor and Jack Imperato.

Frank floored the Cardiff Central man a couple of times, but was then disqualified for hitting him while he was down, having apparently stumbled over his fallen foe. The selectors went for Taylor anyway.

It was only the second edition of the Games, with a comparatively small number of competitors. Frank outpointed a South African, C.B. Hull - in "a hearty head-down toe-to-toe slam", which doesn't sound very Corinthian – and found himself facing the reigning British ABA champion, Jim Rolland, in the semi-final.

Frank Taylor

Frank the policeman in later life

But he outpunched the Scot, the turning point coming when he floored him with a right to the stomach.

The final brought disappointment – and boos from a crowd who thought he had done enough against Australian Leonard Cook. The admittedly partisan *Echo* reporter thought he had landed frequently, despite Cook's "lying-on tactics", with the Aussie being chased all around the ring, "his occasional right clips to the jaw in no way offsetting Taylor's thrusting left-handers". It was little consolation to Frank's older brother, who had driven overnight from Risca in a lorry, or his father, listening to the radio commentary at home.

Taylor, still only 18, moved up to welter the following season, but was stopped on a cut in the Welsh ABA prelims. By the year after, he was a middleweight, where he proceeded to win the title, beating defending champion Alf Ford, from Pontnewynydd, in the semi-final. He found things harder at the British ABAs, being halted by Londoner J.J. McAleer in his first contest.

Frank was described as "a merciless, non-stop fighter" with "a cruel punch", but with the caveat: "If only he would exercise more restraint, he would be a match for anybody in the country."

He did enjoy some success in London, once being credited with a stoppage victory in just four seconds, but the youngster's ring career was nearing its close. With unemployment high in South Wales, police in the English Midlands, in particular, came looking for recruits, with particular attention paid to rugby players and boxers. Indeed, rival Ford had joined the Derby force.

Taylor headed for their neighbours in Nottingham, signing up in August 1936 and serving for 30 years, reaching the rank of sergeant – though he failed his exams for inspector! He remained in the county until his death, at the age of 86.

BILLY THOMAS
(1906-1978)

Welsh Middleweight Champion 1933-35, 1935-36

Australian Welterweight Challenger 1930

You know the saying "Three tries for a Welshman"? Well, it took four attempts before Billy Thomas could call himself a Welsh champion. And he had challenged unsuccessfully for the Australian title as well!

Merthyr-born Thomas moved to the Darran Valley as a youngster and was always announced as from Deri, like big brother Tom. A series of victories in the late 1920s, with top men such as Billy Moore and Glen Moody among his scalps, put him in contention for the national welter crown.

The newly formed Welsh Board matched him with Ammanford veteran Idris Jones – they had already drawn twice - in an eliminator to find a challenger to ruler Ben Marshall. Billy briefly visited the deck in the last, but it was too late to deny him a clear victory. Just to underline his supremacy, he travelled to Jones's home town a couple of weeks later and outscored him again.

Thomas went on to tackle Marshall in Bridgend on October 6, 1928, but found himself on the wrong end of a controversial ruling by referee Billy Morgan. The challenger did well early on, making Ben miss and countering effectively to build a comfortable lead at the halfway mark. The Newport gipsy hit back in the ninth, hooking solidly to the jaw and, in the following session, landed a couple which had Billy in trouble. He clung on desperately

Billy Thomas

as his head cleared and Mr Morgan – whose warning, if any, had been lost in the din – abruptly pulled them apart and disqualified the Bargoed man.

Billy turned his back on the domestic scene and headed Down Under. The Australians loved him, reports describing him as "a superb boxer" and "a versatile customer", and Kiwi fans were equally impressed, especially when he beat local top dog Artie Hay, albeit on a disqualification. Billy began to call himself New Zealand middleweight champion, though nobody there did.

Back across the Tasman, however, the Aussies recognised that their welter belt was on the line when Thomas took on holder Jack Carroll, but a cut eye condemned the visitor to a three-round defeat. Carroll halted him again in a rematch, while Billy never overcame Queenslander Billy Richards despite five attempts. But there were plenty of wins in nearly three years away – and Thomas also returned with a bride, a Scots lass he had met on the boat out.

He was now a middleweight and so was old foe Glen Moody, who by now wore the Welsh crown, and a non-title victory over the Pontypridd man earned Billy a return with the belt on the line. They met at Merthyr Stadium on December 17, 1932, but the challenger strayed below the belt in the fourth and was turfed out. That satisfied nobody, so the pair crossed paths again in Moody's home town three months later; in between, Thomas outpointed the young Tommy Farr, while conceding a stone in weight. Despite that form, Glen took a points decision.

But when the Board ordered a third meeting, Moody decided the proposed purse was less than adequate; the authority promptly stripped him and declared the throne vacant. To decide his successor, Billy faced Ocky Davies in his West Wales fastness at Haverfordwest on January 24, 1934.

That Davies produced what was described as "the greatest fight of his career" and still lost says it all about Thomas's performance. Ocky was constantly on the front foot, but Billy's ringcraft proved too good; the Deri man's neat headwork and fleetness of foot left his rival punching the air, while his straight left was in and out of Ocky's face. Although some partisan locals booed the verdict, the older man's experience had clinched the prize.

It earned Billy a British title eliminator against Scottish champion George Gordon in Manchester, but the heavier Dunblane man won clearly on points.

So Thomas went back to Haverfordwest to give Ocky a second chance. It had the same outcome, even if Billy, cut early on, was less than dominant and relied more on spoiling inside. Once again Davies set the pace and drove forward, but he became wild and left himself open. There were few complaints this time.

When he defended against Ammanford's Danny Evans at Pill Labour Hall on April 29, 1935, Thomas looked jaded, his timing off, and kept slipping over. Evans floored him properly in the sixth and took the verdict. The new holder retired soon afterwards and Billy regained the vacant title at Mountain Ash Pavilion on November 11, 1935, when he outpointed Bunny Eddington, from Pontycymmer. Both men showed plenty of enthusiasm, but the standard of boxing was less than stellar. Eddington, crude, but awkward, provided plenty of problems and Thomas was never able to find his rhythm. He did manage to fell Bunny with a right counter in the fourth,

Billy Thomas in 1955

but that was an isolated success and it was not until the later stages that he pulled away.

His reign lasted barely three months. Facing Dai 'Farmer' Jones, from Johnny Vaughan's all-conquering Ammanford stable, at Swansea's Mannesmann Hall on February 24, 1936. Billy looked apprehensive from the first bell and winced when he shipped a right to the body; from that moment he seemed reluctant to attack and allowed Jones to dictate the exchanges. Thomas survived the second without conviction, but midway through the third a solid right to the jaw sent him down for the full count.

There were a few more outings, but Billy soon turned his attention to training. After the war he set up a gym at Bargoed's Hanbury Hotel and moved into managing and promoting. One of his pupils at Deri ABC, where he was aided by former Markham lightweight Phil Freeman, was two-time Welsh ABA champion Cedric Williams. Billy also trained the Wales team on a visit to Switzerland in 1955.

But his son preferred rugby. Indeed, Billy, Jr, went on to become hooker for Cardiff, collecting two caps for Wales along the way.

TOM THOMAS
(1901-1974)

Welsh Welterweight Champion 1925-27

Thomas James Thomas was damned with faint praise by the pundits of his day. "Not over-clever," they sniffed, "but one of the determined sort, who generally gets there".

Well, not everyone can be blessed with outstanding talent, in boxing or elsewhere. And, for the vast majority of us, a stubborn dedication to making the best of what we are given is something to be admired. Certainly, Welsh fans at the time had every respect for the Deri man who ruled their welterweights for two years.

Tom spent his first few years in Merthyr, before the family moved to the Darran valley. He first laced on the gloves as World War I drew to its close, but took some time to find success. He began "getting there" in the early 1920s, building his reputation across South Wales, once flattening the same man twice in a night: a Cardiffian called Young Keepings, knocked out inside a round in the opening bout of the evening, pleaded for a second chance – and Thomas did it again!

He then headed for Belfast, Manchester and the revered National Sporting Club, whose powers-that-be were impressed enough to match him in a British welterweight eliminator against Tommy Milligan on April 7, 1924. It proved brief, but entertaining, one of the most exciting slugfests the dinner-jacketed patrons had ever seen. The pair went toe to toe from the first bell, but the Scot simply hit harder. He floored Thomas four times in the opener and then, early in the second, bundled him through the ropes to be counted out as he tried to regain the ring. Milligan went on to rule Britain, Europe and the Empire at both welter and middle; his victim focussed on domestic honours.

He was already being referred to as Welsh welter champion, even before he outpointed Caerphilly's Martin Sampson, a former victim, over 20 rounds at Newport, a bout he later suggested had earned him the crown. But these were two-minute sessions and

Tom Thomas

172

therefore not eligible for title status. The scrap saw a little bit of history, however: rugby international Jerry Shea, recently retired from the ring, made his bow as a referee.

Tom's claim gained the official stamp of approval with a narrow points victory over Billy Green, from Taffs Well, on August 21, 1926, at Milford Haven, where Thomas had introduced himself with a couple of wins in previous weeks. With the reputations both enjoyed as bangers, few expected it to go the full 20, but the pair showed they also had solid chins as they withstood each other's bombardment.

Green started quickly, but Tom's neater boxing caught the eye and it was Billy's sturdiness that was put to the test as the contest developed. At the end Cardiff referee Fred Good went for Thomas as the new king. Not

Stow Hill Pavilion, where Tom was dethroned by Ben Marshall

an undisputed monarch: there were several unwilling to bow the knee - Billy Moore and Kid Thomas notable among them - but Tom Thomas and Green were the only men to have met at the weight and over the full championship distance.

Moore, a Penygraig publican who once wore the lightweight belt, was given his chance, but the Milford crowd were as frustrated as the Rhondda man when an exciting set-to ended in his disqualification. Thomas began strongly, but a clip to the side of the head sent him briefly to the canvas in the third, although he seemed more off-balance than hurt.

There was no such confusion early in the fourth, when Tom dropped to his knees under a volley of blows, holding the bottom rope with one hand. Moore, for all his vast experience, raced in impatiently and struck Thomas to the head, forcing referee Bob Hill to rule him out. Billy, sportingly, addressed the fans and apologised for his transgression.

Thus reprieved, Tom retained the crown for another six months, but was then dethroned by the Newport gipsy, Ben Marshall. They met at the Pavilion Theatre on Stow Hill, in the challenger's home town, on March 22, 1927, and even though the local man had to lose a surplus pound beforehand, he always looked likely to prevail.

As early as the second, Thomas was down from a two-fisted attack and, despite some game defiance, was felled again in the sixth, the blow also cutting Tom near the left eye. The injury clearly hampered the holder and although he survived two more knockdowns in the seventh, he was pulled out at the bell to end the session.

That was that as far as titles were concerned. Tom kept going for a few more years, but left home to build a new life in Southampton, where he married Antonetta, the daughter of an Italian book repairer, and earned a crust in a bedding factory.

NOEL TRIGG
(1934-)

Welsh Light-Heavyweight Champion 1956-58

When the young soldier from the Maindee area of Newport stepped on a booby trap in Korea it seemed to spell the end of a promising ring career. Noel Trigg could see nothing following the explosion – and he remained blind for a week, being nursed slowly back to health in a Canadian hospital.

Before being called up for his National Service, Noel had mixed two widely different sports. His day job involved caring for the bowling greens at the Lysaght Institute; by night he wore the colours of Pill ABC to a British schoolboy title. Twice Trigg lost points decisions to future heavyweight ace Joe Erskine, who claimed he had never before been hit so hard. But that power also led to tragedy: knockout victim Gordon Avery, also from Cardiff, never recovered consciousness and died in hospital.

Noel turned pro in 1952 with local newsagent Joe Carr, while Billy Taylor and weight-lifter Dennis Bartlett looked after his training, and won his first 11 fights. But it was hardly straightforward. In Trigg's second contest, Watford's Sid Cain broke his jaw with a first-round knockdown; Noel ignored it to take a six-round decision. Three months later Cornishman Stephen Coombes did the same. Once again the injured party survived to have his arm raised.

Noel was soon in line for honours and faced reigning Welsh light-heavy boss Ken Rowlands before 30,000 at Maindy Stadium on May 7, 1956. The tall Rowlands, Maerdy-born, but Luton-raised, was a hot favourite, but was never able to establish his elegant left lead as the challenger worked inside and did enough to earn the nod after a disappointing encounter.

Phil Edwards, a 20-year-old middleweight from Cardiff, overcame a six-pound deficit to outclass Trigg and take a £200 sidestake before a packed house at Sophia Gardens Pavilion. It was not the best confidence booster for Noel's first defence, at the same venue on March 18, 1957, with Penarth trier Don Sainsbury in the other corner. Six months older, but with fewer bouts, Sainsbury could also point to a win over Rowlands.

Noel Trigg

The holder began confidently, dictating the pace, although rocked by an uppercut late in the opener. Trigg's right hand was repeatedly landing, but the fourth saw an enforced change in tactics: the middle knuckle on that busy fist gave way, leaving Noel to rely on the left for the remaining eight rounds. Don staged a late onslaught, the champion defending desperately on the ropes at times, but it was the Newportonian's brave resistance which found favour with referee Joe Morgan, whose decision received a mixed reception from the 3,000 crowd.

The hand damage sidelined Trigg for a year, but he proved the fractured mitt was fine again when he used it to knock out former British middleweight kingpin Albert Finch in three rounds, a defeat which prompted the Croydon man to hang up his gloves. Surprisingly, Trigg would not be that far behind him.

On April 23, 1958, Noel found himself back at Sophia Gardens to risk the throne against Redvers Sangoe, who could point to a stoppage win over Sainsbury in an official eliminator. The muscular Butetown boy proved too strong for Trigg – who had always struggled to put on weight rather than shed it - in the sort of tussle where bulk was as important as technique. Noel, widely tipped to keep his belt, began well, but Sangoe settled into the scrap and gradually took control of an encounter which had too much wrestling to be a classic. At the final bell, the Cardiffian was crowned the new champion of Wales.

The former ruler gave up his job as a railway fireman to base himself in London as a full-time boxer, training at the Fulham football ground, but it was a gamble that saw him floored and outpointed by both former Lonsdale Belt challenger Arthur Howard and newly arrived Canadian Burke Emery.

When ex-British champion Alex Buxton visited the Stow Hill Drill Hall – the only time Trigg boxed in Newport as a pro – he put Noel on the deck three times, but the local man recovered to drop Buxton, only for those fragile eyebrows to force his corner to retire him at the end of the fourth. When a further inch-long gash brought a premature end to a clash with Brummie Gordon Corbett, it was enough for Noel, who opted for the safe side of the ropes.

Back in Wales, he ran the Coach and Horses at Caerwent – where he added a gym and trained local youngsters - and then had a smallholding before moving to Gibraltar for three years. On his return to Newport, he built and ran The Gladiator in Malpas for seven years. Even when he had placed the tea towels over the pumps for good, it was not to sit back in front of the television.

Noel was elected to Gwent County Council and then to Newport City Council, where he served as mayor in 2008, before retiring from politics at the age of 81.

ROBBIE TURLEY
(1986-)

- Commonwealth Super-Bantamweight Champion 2017-

- Welsh Super-Bantamweight Champion 2011-12

- Celtic Super-Bantamweight Champion 2012

The scenes of jubilation at the Newport Centre were tinged with relief. Robbie Turley had halted former holder Bobby Jenkinson to claim the vacant Commonwealth super-bantam title. But for a while it had seemed his career was to suffer a premature ending.

The blond lad from Cefn Fforest – he lived in the next street to future world champion Nathan Cleverly – had just won the Celtic belt when a routine scan revealed that a cyst on his brain had changed colour. Always wary of such occurrences, even though nobody could be sure it would put him at any greater risk, the Board promptly pulled his licence.

It took two years – and a considerable outlay on medical and legal expertise – before he was allowed back in the ring. No wonder Turley was ecstatic when he finally won a major honour.

Having started boxing at 10, Robbie was good enough to represent Wales at European championships and Commonwealth Games, though going out in his first bout each time. His defeat in Melbourne came the night after his girlfriend had rung to say she had lost their baby; they were to have a son the following year, but at 10 days old he was rushed to hospital. Turley was due to contest a Welsh ABA semi-final the following day and when the Welsh ABA refused to reschedule the bout he turned pro in disgust.

Managed by Chris Sanigar and trained by Tony Borg, Robbie won six of his first seven and was matched with Dai Davies for the vacant Welsh feather throne at Newport. The experienced Merthyr man was well on top when a cut prompted the stoppage at the end of the ninth.

But Turley had better fortune down at super-bantam, where he took on North Walian Paul Economides on February 5, 2011, and took a wide points decision to the

Robbie Turley with his Commonwealth belt

Turley (right) halts Gavin Reid to win the Celtic title

delight of his Newport Centre fan club, with their trademark chant of "We know Robbie Turl". It earned the new champion a chance to tackle unbeaten Ulsterman Carl Frampton for his Celtic belt. The future world ruler emerged with a unanimous decision, but all at Cardiff's Motorpoint Arena acknowledged that Turley had given him all the problems he could handle.

With Frampton moving on to bigger things, Robbie stepped up to claim the vacant Celtic throne, returning to the Motorpoint on February 2, 2012, to halt Scot Gavin Reid in six rounds. Then came his enforced exile from the sport.

Two rust-removers when he reappeared led to another shot at Dai Davies, this time in the holder's Merthyr stronghold, and after Turley was pulled out at the end of the eighth he decided to drop back to super-bantam.

The wisdom of the move was demonstrated when he produced the most dominant display of his career in widely outpointing Devonian Jamie Speight in a British title eliminator in Bristol, but the promised shot at the Lonsdale Belt seemed as far away as ever.

Robbie was kept waiting for the whole of 2015 – and was then told he had to box a final eliminator against unbeaten Durham traveller Tommy Ward at Houghton-le-Spring on March 5, 2016. The local established early control and when Turley was docked a point in the seventh for holding it put things pretty much beyond reach, even though a late surge narrowed the deficit to six, four and two points.

Robbie displays his other talent – as a singer

For a while it seemed Robbie, a talented singer, might seek his fortune in showbiz after winning the Voice of the Valleys talent show, but then came the clash with Jenkinson at the Newport Centre on April 7, 2017. Originally an eliminator, if was upgraded to a vacant title fight when Gamal Yafai, who had dethroned the Lincoln warrior, relinquished.

Turley looked tense in the opener, when his timing was awry, but a flash knockdown in the second – Bobby claimed a push, but referee Victor Loughlin counted - eased the nerves and the next few sessions were hard fought and competitive. By the sixth, however, the Welshman was in control and when, in the ninth, a right to the body dropped the tiring visitor, the towel floated in from the Jenkinson corner.

It had taken 10 years, but for the new Commonwealth king, all the trials and tribulations had proved worthwhile.

IAN TURNER
(1975-)

🥊 Welsh Bantamweight Champion 1997-99

Most people hope to acquire wisdom. For the lanky bantamweight from Tredegar, it was the reverse. Wisdom teeth in his case, of course. Constant problems with the mouldy molars plagued Ian Turner's early career. Each time he had to have one extracted it meant several weeks on the sidelines; manager Dai Gardiner calculated that his man had missed out on eight fights before the last was removed.

But between visits to the dentist, Turner had still managed to collect a Welsh title and put himself into contention for a Lonsdale Belt.

Ian learned his trade with Tommy Evans at the Heads of the Valleys club in Ebbw Vale, becoming Welsh ABA bantam champion before the trainers' dispute that split the Welsh amateur scene meant he was unable to defend his championship. So Ian turned pro with Gardiner, Evans continuing in charge of the gym work. Turner made his bow with a points success over former amateur conqueror Henry Jones and added a couple of wins and a draw – against first-timer Dave Travers on hostile territory at Wolverhampton – before the two rivals met again with the vacant Welsh 8st 6lb crown up for grabs.

They faced each other on neutral ground beneath the garish paintings of Swansea's Brangwyn Hall on December 2, 1997. Neither man had travelled beyond six rounds, so a steady start was perhaps to be expected, but the taller Gwent fighter began to take control with his jab. Jones, from Pembroke, worked his way inside to some effect in the middle sessions, when Ian picked up a cut over the left eye.

Ian Turner

With the experienced Gardiner keeping the bleeding under control, Turner regained the ascendancy before rocking Henry with a left uppercut midway through the eighth. A couple of rights landed before Jones touched down and, although the West Walian rose at six and attempted

Turner is tended to in the corner by manager Dai Gardiner

to battle back, when he shipped another big right referee Mike Heatherwick stepped in to indicate a new champion.

A decision over former Midlands super-bantam ruler Matthew Harris boosted Turner's name recognition across the border and his reputation was enhanced further when he went to Oldham and drew with ex-British fly boss Ady Lewis.

It was a result duly noted by the powers-that-be, who ordered a rematch with official eliminator status. The Welshman was also offered a short-notice trip to South Africa to face holder Simon Ramoni for the fringe IBO belt. The invitation was declined.

There were problems with the Lewis eliminator, too. Scot Tommy Gilmour wanted to stage it at Carlisle, but the money – with a 60-40 winner-loser split – meant that if Turner lost he would earn less for 10 rounds than he had for eight in their first meeting. Instead he decided to stay in Wales – and jump up two divisions.

The national featherweight throne was unoccupied and Gardiner matched Ian with blond Cardiffian David Morris at the capital's Welsh Institute of Sport on February 23, 1999. Morris, a former Welsh ABA king, had a statistically unimpressive record since changing codes, but had faced a string of top men including two future world champions in fellow-townsman Barry Jones and Glasgow's Scott Harrison.

Turner had the technical ability, but the local man, in his first paid outing on home ground, had the will. Ian would control the opening minute of each session, but Morris inexorably forced him back and kept the pressure on for the remainder. Turner's defence was solid, but he was being outworked and David, superbly conditioned by former British title

Still using the hook to good effect - fisherman Ian floors a sturgeon

challenger Harry Carroll, kept up his torrid pace to earn a 97-94 vote from Mr Heatherwick.

Strangely, Morris never boxed again. His victim, however, kept going for another four years, but that was largely a business decision. He won a couple of four-rounders, but was outpointed by the likes of future world title challenger Esham Pickering, Commonwealth ruler Brian Carr, WBU bantam boss Johnny Armour and, in Spain, unbeaten prospect Germán Guartos.

When the points defeats turned into stoppages – three in a row, against British title challenger Jim Betts, future WBU and European champion Steve Foster, Jr, and unbeaten Yorkshireman Danny Wallace – it was time to hang up the gloves and give more time to his passion for fishing.

Not that machinist Turner has walked away from the sport entirely. He still trains at the Heads of the Valleys gym and if head coach Mel Hamer needs someone to spar with the kids he knows who to ask!

PAT WARBURTON
(1911-1960)

🥊 Welsh Flyweight Champion 1936-38

Patrick Warburton was the product of harsh times. Born in a terraced house at Waunllwyd, just down the valley from Ebbw Vale, he was the eighth child of miner James and his wife Ellen – yet only three of those siblings lived long enough to greet their baby brother.

Boxing was one route out of such an environment, providing not merely a few extra pounds in the wallet, but the opportunity to start a new life in more prosperous surroundings. In due course, it took the Monmouthshire youngster to London, but first he had to demonstrate his worth at home. A string of victories achieved that, notably two decisions over Al 'Kid' McCoy, an Argoed lad whose real name was Joseph Albert Poole, with only a controversial disqualification loss to Tredegar boy Kid Leyland marring his record. The run earned him his first invitation to display his wares in the imperial capital.

The metropolitan experts were impressed as he compiled another winning streak, his only setback coming when he travelled to Glasgow's famous Kelvin Hall to tackle the bigger Willie McCamley. Warburton, only 7st 8lb at the weigh-in to the Scot's 8st 2lb, paid the price when McCamley took the verdict after 10 rounds.

There was one trip home as well, to face old foe McCoy in a Welsh flyweight eliminator at the White City – a greyhound track in Cardiff - on May 6, 1935, part of a week's events to mark the silver jubilee of King George V. Much was expected of the Ebbw Vale man, given the reports emanating from London, but the Welsh fans were to be disappointed. With McCoy less than keen to open up, Pat found his all-out onslaughts frustrated to a large degree, effort not being matched by precision. There was no doubt about his right to the decision, but observers saw little to worry titleholder Charlie Hazel.

Illness prevented Warburton from capitalising on his victory over McCoy with a shot at the belt, which Hazel

Pat Warburton

had now relinquished, so the authorities upgraded the other eliminator, between Cardiffian Ken Barrett and London-based Herbie Hill, to a full title fight, on condition the winner – it turned out to be Hill - faced the Ebbw Vale man once he was restored to health.

As Pat moved up in class defeats became more frequent, with future European challenger Tiny Baldock and ringwise Stoke southpaw Tut Whalley among his conquerors, but the most painful came when he was given the dubious honour of a place in the opposite corner when Benny Lynch, already flyweight champion of the world, made his London debut at the Stadium Club, Holborn. The bout was scheduled for nine rounds to comply with a new Board rule that nobody could box two contests of 30 minutes' duration within four days. The fact that Lynch had won the previous bout in four rounds apparently had no bearing, but the whole hoo-hah proved academic as the hard-hitting little Scot despatched Warburton in three, including six knockdowns.

The experience clearly did not have any long-term effects as Warburton's next venture through the ropes brought him the Welsh title. He found it difficult to land a glove on holder Hill in the early stages on August 3, 1936, but dropped him briefly in the third. The bank holiday crowd at Swansea's Vetch Field saw Pat take total control against a tiring champion, flooring him twice in the seventh and twice more in the eighth, when referee C.B. Thomas stepped in to end it just as the bell sounded.

Now permanently based in London, it was one of Warburton's last appearances in his native land. Even a title defence against that man McCoy the following April took place at Holborn, where Pat defied a badly cut eye to outlast a challenger whose only joy came from occasional in-fighting.

There was little left in the way of celebration. Four stoppage losses in succession ended the pre-war part of Warburton's career, but he returned in 1946 with three wins, only to be halted twice by Ronnie Bishop, a Markham boy and himself a former Welsh flyweight champion. The second loss ended his career: Bishop knocked him through the ropes and Pat was counted out while lying on the floor of Watford Town Hall.

He was not to enjoy a long retirement, dying in London 13 years later at the age of 48.

ANDY WILLIAMS
(1965-2013)

🥊 Welsh Lightweight Champion 1986-87

In the closing decades of the last century a fight for the Welsh lightweight title pretty much guaranteed thrills and spills. From the all-Merthyr epic between Johnny Wall and Martyn Galleozzie to veteran Cardiffian Mervyn Bennett's defiant stand against unbeaten Monmouth youngster Gareth Jordan, battles for the domestic 9st 9lb crown produced some of the best fistic entertainment on offer.

Between those classics, a talented southpaw from Garndiffaith played his part in maintaining the tradition. Andy Williams showed his skills from an early age: he won five Welsh schools championships and twice converted them into British titles before his only attempt at the senior Welsh ABAs saw him outpointed in the final by Llanelli's Neil Haddock, a future British pro champion.

Williams took the plunge with local manager Jack Evans, yet it could

Andy Williams

hardly be said that he hit the ground running – there were just two wins in his first seven fights – and Andy made a brave decision after being cut and stopped in Scotland by unbeaten Alex Dickson, later to wear the British lightweight crown. He packed in his job at the Royal Ordnance Factory at Glascoed and became a full-time fighter.

His reward was not long delayed. On April 28, 1986, at a delirious STAR Leisure Centre in Cardiff, the Gwent youngster, still only 20, won the vacant Welsh lightweight title with a repeat points victory over local trier Mark Pearce, whom he had outscored at Blaenavon five months earlier.

Andy's right lead was rarely out of Pearce's face, although a lack of power allowed the city man to remain competitive, particularly when his tormentor took something of a breather in the middle sessions. Mark staged a desperate rally in the last, but Williams withstood the storm and a three-punch combination sent Pearce's gumshield flying into the press seats. Caerleon referee Adrian Morgan had four rounds between them at the close, when fans hurled "nobbings" into the ring in appreciation of a memorable encounter; the new champion generously handed his share of the money to his gallant rival.

Finding his first challenger was not difficult. Unbeaten Swansea puncher Keith Parry had stopped four in a row before they met at Ebbw Vale Leisure Centre and came within seconds of making it five in a clash which stood out even among Welsh lightweight deciders.

Williams's wrong-way-round stance seemed at first to baffle Parry, who had never before faced the problem, and early in the third Andy uncorked a right which felled Keith, shaking him again before the gong. The champion's inability to apply the coup de grace allowed the long-haired challenger - only 22, but still two years the older man - to recover, and he began to score his share,

Williams (right) under pressure from Keith Parry in their first Welsh title showdown

bringing blood from an old scar on the Monmouthshire fighter's nose.

A little extra-curricular activity at the end of the sixth drew stern words from the third man, again Adrian Morgan, but the champion's mobility kept him out of serious trouble until the eighth, when he shipped a left hook that put him on the deck. Williams winked encouragingly at his corner before clambering up at seven, but Parry was given new heart and kept up the pressure.

The ninth saw a twisting left to the midriff send Andy down again and Mr Morgan took a long look before accepting the boxer's insistent claims that he could continue. It was the correct decision: Williams kept away from the left until the bell and even resumed the offensive in the last to take a clear verdict.

Williams was called up for a British title eliminator against former conqueror Dickson in Scotland, but heavy snow caused a postponement and when it was rearranged, a different Scot, Ian McLeod, dropped Andy with a body shot in the third and earned a wide margin on referee Sid Nathan's card.

Andy works out on the heavy bag

It was back to domestic business for Andy, who faced Parry again at Swansea's Mayfair Suite on October 28, 1987, and it signalled a changing of the guard. Keith floored Williams with a right to the head in the second and hammered away in the third until Andy's skill and mobility gained him temporary control. This time, however, the local was willing to take a few to get inside and the sixth saw him in total command.

Williams slipped over early in the eighth, but was then poleaxed by a left to the jaw, which sent him swivelling on his heels before crashing beneath the bottom rope. Somehow he made it to his feet, but the referee – once more Mr Morgan – waved it off and crowned a new monarch.

Andy took 16 months out, reappearing somewhat sporadically for another two years, but winning only once, in what turned out to be his final contest, against Pembroke journeyman Mike Morrison on the outskirts of Swansea. His life in retirement was a sad one in which he struggled with alcohol before dying of cancer at the early age of 47.

ANEURIN WILLIAMS
(1960-)

🥊 Welsh Light-Heavyweight Champion 1983-86

Monmouthshire's greatest son, Aneurin Bevan, the founder of the National Health Service, died of cancer in the summer of 1960. A few days earlier, a new-born baby had been named in his honour. And Aneurin Williams was to make his mark, too, though in a totally different sphere.

The young bricklayer from Gilwern found his vocation in the boxing ring, learning the trade with trainer Gordon Davies at the Semtex club in Brynmawr and claiming two Welsh ABA titles while still a teenager. The pro scene beckoned and Davies sent him to the man who had guided his own career, the incomparable Eddie Thomas.

Nye made his pro bow on a Colin Jones undercard in Merthyr, edging out Londoner Lee White, and won his next three before Jamaican-born Brummie Antonio Harris survived a fifth-round left hook to take a clear decision. The Welshman was back on the right side of the result next time with a two-round demolition of Scot Gary Jones, but two more West Indians outpointed him, one a future British title challenger, Keith Bristol.

But three victories on the spin earned the Gwent man a place in one corner when the vacant Welsh light-heavy title was disputed at Ebbw Vale Leisure Centre on October 27, 1983. The opposite stool was occupied by Chris Lawson, a greenkeeper at Cardigan Golf Club and a former holder. Both came in a couple of pounds over the limit, but were able to shed the surplus in time.

The bulk of the highly vocal support was behind Williams, having travelled the comparatively short journey along the A465, and they were on their feet as their man stormed out seeking an early finish. Lawson coolly

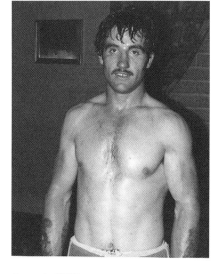

Aneurin Williams

187

survived the onslaught and a few West Wales accents began to be heard as he came more into things.

Nye targeted the body to good effect in the middle rounds, but was often wild and Chris ended the sixth with a solid left that caused a little uncertainty in the eyes of the Monmouthshire man. Trying to capitalise, Lawson opened the seventh with a series of left hooks which had Williams covering up, but the Cardigan fighter was unable to sustain the pace and after a further head-to-head exchange Nye winked at his rival before they returned to their corners.

There was little let-up in the last two sessions, an even ninth followed by a lung-busting effort by Lawson which earned him the last, amid a constant din from the opposing fans. But it was the home crowd with the final cheers, referee Adrian Morgan having Williams two rounds up at the finish. His success brought an extra thrill for trainer Davies, whose own Welsh title shot, at lightweight 20 years earlier, ended in frustration when he was held to a draw by Cardiffian holder Teddy Best.

It was to be the last time the new champion came out on top. There was a draw with Scouser Bernie Kavanagh, but five defeats, all lost on points over eight rounds. Two came against former conqueror Harris and British title challenger Trevor Cattouse, while Nye's final contests came on foreign shores. Former WBA cruiser challenger John Odhiambo prevailed in Italy, while in Bordeaux Rufino Angulo was given the nod despite being floored in the last; the verdict was roundly booed by the locals.

The fortunate Angulo went on to have two shots at world belts. Williams never boxed again. But he has never gone far from the fight game and is still involved as a trainer at the Heads of the Valleys gym in Ebbw Vale.

J.T. WILLIAMS
(1970-2016)

🥊 **Commonwealth Super-Featherweight Challenger 1994**

🥊 **Welsh Super-Featherweight Champion 1993-95**

Every so often, whispers drift through the boxing scene. Someone a bit special is on the way. The hardcore followers nudge each other and pass on the latest name to look out for. And, if the lad in question can bang a bit, the news spreads like lightning.

So it was with Miah-John Williams, from Cwmbran. The first part of his name honoured grandfather Jeremiah Williams, a one-time booth fighter. More recently, father Tony had been a useful flyweight who now ran the Pontypool and Panteg club where his son threw his first punches. Young John was soon wearing their vest to Welsh titles at schoolboy and youth level.

It was the Gaelic Games of 1986 which first brought him to the notice of a wider audience. He won the gold with two first-round victories, the semi-final success coming over a young Ulsterman. Wayne McCullough went on to become WBC bantamweight champion and was not stopped again for 20 years.

Perhaps that passed most English observers by. But when Williams won the National Association of Boys' Clubs' tournament three years later, halting all three foes, it made him the talk of the town, with his 20-second demolition job in the final given exposure on TV.

Life as a senior proved harder: he reached two British ABA finals, but finished second, while a shot at the Commonwealth Games brought defeat by the eventual silver medallist. Londoner Frank Maloney, remembering those junior triumphs, signed him up, while Dad continued in the corner. The existence of a Birmingham light-heavy of the same name meant John called himself J.T. Williams for his new career.

J.T. Williams

A debut draw was followed by four straight wins before Hull veteran Steve Pollard collected an upset points win in London, a loss which prompted Williams to leave Maloney for Welshman Dai Gardiner. He still appeared on a Maloney show when he faced British super-feather king Neil Haddock in a non-title 10-rounder on the undercard of the Lennox Lewis-Frank

Father and son - Young John with trainer and mentor Tony

Bruno showdown at the National Stadium. John lost by a three-round margin, but did well enough to earn a crack at the Welsh throne Haddock had previously occupied.

The Llanelli man had been succeeded by another fighter from the tinplate town, Barrie Kelley, and he and Williams – former amateur sparring partners who shared a mutual dislike - met at the Rhondda Leisure Centre on November 10, 1993. This time J.T. had his arm raised, but the whole affair was far from conclusive.

Kelley had been inactive since winning the belt 10 months previously, ruled out by surgery on his right hand, and the rust was clear at the start. Williams took the opener, but Barrie edged the second before the outcome was decided early in the third. Their heads came together, leaving the champion bleeding profusely from a cut along his left eyebrow. By the end of the session, the damage was so bad that Kelley's manager, former heavyweight Billy Aird, signalled his retirement.

Williams, (right) on the attack against British champion Neil Haddock

There was talk of a shot at the watching Haddock, but fellow-Welshman Floyd Havard was first in that queue and Williams turned his attention to the Commonwealth crown, won by beanpole Canadian Tony Pep at Cardiff's National Sports Centre two years earlier. Pep – whose Irish-born manager, Patrick Connaughton, would later settle and promote in Cardiff – returned to Britain to face J.T. at the York Hall on July 30, 1994.

By now former England amateur captain Graham Moughton was calling the shots in the corner, but it mattered little. Just 92 seconds after the first bell, Williams's bid to be the first Welshman to win the 9st 4lb title was over. Pep took half a minute to check out his rival, before suddenly stepping up the pace; a left hook-cum-uppercut shook John and a follow-up onslaught sent him to the canvas. The challenger bravely stormed back in, but Pep bided his time until launching a succession of head shots which dropped his man once more. This time, when he rose, referee John Coyle called a halt.

Despite employing a hypnotherapist in a bid to rebuild his conference, Williams found himself thinking of the Pep fight as he walked to the ring to defend his Welsh crown on March 8, 1995. It explained a hesitant start against North Walian warrior Eddie Lloyd beneath the chandeliers of Cardiff's City Hall.

The champion gradually caught up with the 31-year-old Lloyd, who spent his summers running a string of donkeys on the beach at Rhyl, but the older man was supremely fit and held his own in a thrilling encounter. J.T. had Eddie on the ropes for much of the eighth and ninth, but Lloyd rocked and cut his man in the last. Referee Ivor Bassett scored a draw.

Williams knocked out lanky Brummie Norman Dhalie with a body shot on a pre-Christmas show at the Helmaen Club, outside Usk, but personal problems brought an early end to his career. He was to die prematurely, as well, suffering three heart attacks in hospital following treatment for a hip injury, an inquest jury returning a verdict of misadventure. The former teenage sensation was just 45.

CRAIG WOODRUFF
(1992-)

🥊 **Welsh Lightweight Champion 2013**

The six-foot lightweight they called, with a degree of irony, 'Smiler' won the Welsh title in just his fifth pro outing. But then his career seemed to grind to a halt.

That talent was obvious when the 15-year-old first visited the gym near his home in the Alway area of Newport. Former British champion Steve Sims guided him through a decent amateur career which included victories over Commonwealth medallist Mo Nasir and future Olympian Joe Cordina.

He was only 19 when he joined the paid ranks, with Sims still at the helm, and made his debut on a big Matchroom show in Liverpool. Eddie Hearn's organisation had close connections with Poland and Craig was invited as the fall guy for another teenager, European junior semi-finalist Konrad Dabrowski, also dipping his toes into the professional pond. Woodruff ditched the script and won a clear decision.

Craig Woodruff

On home ground there were mixed fortunes, with Craig taking all four rounds against Llanelli boy Liam Ellis, but losing all four against locally trained rival Mitch Buckland. A trip to Yorkshire saw him step up to six to face former British super-feather king Carl Johanneson; despite conceding six pounds, the Newport lad took the spoils and the loser promptly announced his retirement.

Woodruff, on the other hand, was matched for a title shot of his own, facing Talbot Green crowd-pleaser Tony Pace at the Newport Centre on February 23, 2013. There was confusion as to whether Pace's recent win over Cynon Valley man Lance Sheehan had involved the Welsh honour along with the so-called British Masters belt, but either way it was up for grabs on this occasion.

On the back of that success, Pace was expected to prevail, but things proved very different. Woodruff belied his youth and lack of experience with a superb performance, a mongoose seeing off 'The Snake' with confidence and control. While mostly leaning away from Tony's assaults and responding with sharp counters, Craig also held his own when drawn into the sort of exchanges that had seen Pace dubbed "the Welsh Gatti".

He was well clear on referee Wynford Jones's card at halfway, when the Mid-Glamorgan man began to flag. Normally an all-action scrapper, he had apparently been less than diligent in making weight and the sixth saw him focussed entirely on defence. Realising there was little left in the tank, veteran mentor Dai Gardiner pulled Tony out at the end of the session.

A drop to super-feather brought Woodruff an impressive fourth-round knockout of the ringwise Dai Davies before he faced his sole conqueror, Buckland, for the vacant Celtic lightweight throne. Mitch built an early lead, but Craig came to life in the fourth and it was nip and tuck from then on, something seemingly lost on the judges, who favoured Buckland by three, four and an incredible eight points. To add to his misery, Woodruff, having lost to a fellow-countryman under championship conditions, was stripped of his Welsh title.

The following year saw 'Smiler' revert to the role of "opponent". After running out of steam against unbeaten traveller Martin Joseph Ward and needing rescue in the fourth, Craig had paid only three visits to the gym in a matter of months when he had the call, at eight days' notice, to tackle Olympic champion Luke Campbell in Liverpool. His lack of fitness restricted his ambition, but he caused the golden boy a fair few problems over six rounds and the whitewash 60-54 scoreline owed more to the Hull youngster's reputation than what he actually achieved on the night.

Instead of serving as a boost, that display marked the end – for the moment – of the Newport youngster's career. Fatherhood and night shifts at Wilkinson's took him away from the sport, while a court appearance following a football field brawl ended with a suspended prison term and a spell of community service; his licence was automatically withdrawn until these were completed.

HARRY WOODS
(1975-)

WBC International Flyweight Challenger 1996

Harry Woods had started his Christmas celebrations early with a few drinks at a friend's house when fellow-boxer Shayne Webb turned up with news that his father, Harry's trainer Malcolm, needed to see him urgently. The Bargoed boy rushed over to hear that he had been offered a fight for the WBC International title two weeks later – in Ghana!

Instead of enjoying the festivities with his family, he spent the big day shedding surplus weight and getting sharp before facing unbeaten prospect Alex 'Ali' Baba. An attempt to go for a run saw 80 children chasing him along the road, so training was limited to skipping and pad work in the hotel. But it worked.

When the pair came together in Accra on December 28, 1996, it was a war, with the referee able to take a watching brief as the fighters stood toe to toe for 12 rounds. The African's extra class earned him the verdict, but the legendary Azumah Nelson, commentating at ringside, was fulsome in his praise of the Welshman's efforts. Yet, while Baba went on to a WBC title bid, Harry's future held only disappointment.

As a pupil at Webb's Aberbargoed ABC, Caerphilly-born Woods – actually Wood, but an extra 's' was somehow acquired - amassed a collection of national age-group vests before repeating the success at senior level, although flu ruled him out of a British semi-final against future world champion Paul Ingle. His chance to defend the Welsh title was scuppered when he came in overweight and he opted to turn pro with Dai Gardiner.

Harry Woods

There were two draws in his first three bouts, one despite floooring unbeaten Swansea chef Mark Hughes, and the pair were set for a Welsh title rematch only for a retina problem to bring a premature end to Hughes's career. There was a further setback when Harry suffered his first loss, a controversial disqualification against Blackpool-based Scot Louis Veitch at the Rhondda Fach Sports Centre. Referee Mike Heatherwick called on the pair to stop boxing after Veitch lost his mouthpiece, but he was so far away that Woods, well on top, never heard the instruction and proceeded to flatten the veteran, who was unable to continue.

Harry had better luck with Mr Heatherwick when the Maesteg official gave him the verdict over the heavier Matthew Harris in a fight the Brummie looked to have edged. Right or wrong, the win underlined the Rhymney Valley lad's British title claims and a proposed meeting with Lancastrian Adi Lewis looked set to be recognised as an official eliminator. But champion Mickey Cantwell, booked for a WBO fly bid, gave up the Lonsdale Belt and Lewis was matched with Scot Keith Knox to decide his successor, much to the annoyance of manager Gardiner.

The short-notice Christmas safari to Ghana came as some consolation. But if the result there was half-expected, Harry's next fight brought a hammer blow. Spaniard José Antonio López Bueno arrived at a chilly National Ice Rink – half the arena was closed off and behind a curtain the ice was uncovered - on the back of three straight losses. But the waiter from Zaragoza made Harry miss frequently and landed regular rights, one of which brought blood streaming down the Welshman's face in the fifth. Referee Heatherwick - that man again – called a halt and Woods needed five stitches in his left eyebrow.

The unexpected victory proved a turning point for López Bueno, who went on to capture the WBO fly crown. For Harry it marked the beginning of the end. Disillusionment, plus a foot injury caused when he dropped a scaffolding pole, extended the break to more than a year before he reappeared at Ebbw Vale with a routine win over fight centurion Des Gargano.

But two points losses to Londoner Stephen Oates bookended a trip to Spain and an outing on one of López Bueno's world title undercards. Woods twice floored unbeaten Dmitri Kirilov, later to occupy the IBF super-fly throne, but the Russian teenager was handed a disputed, if unanimous, decision.

The slide continued, with the writing clearly on the wall when Woods was beaten by dreadlocked southpaw Frankie de Milo, a Rwandan refugee who secured Swedish citizenship before settling in Bristol. Woods had dislocated his right shoulder two weeks earlier and should not have boxed; the injury proved too much and he was on the receiving end for several rounds before being pulled out at the end of the sixth.

Harry was determined not to leave boxing on such a note and, after an eight-month break, he looked sharp as he outpointed Dubliner Willie Valentine in Plymouth. But the shoulder was still a problem and he never laced up the gloves again.

Now settled at Fleur-de-Lys with his partner and their three children, Harry admits he was never as professional as he might have been, content to get by on natural talent. But he can still look back on the time he earned the respect of Africa's greatest fighter.

The day after th night before - Har and conqueror Al Baba in Accra

SUPPORTING CAST

While the principal actors have been profiled in the main pages of this book, there are thousands of other performers worthy of mention. Here we give a nod to just a few.

Some came close to individual inclusion, notably Gary Cooper, robbed of a Welsh title because officials did not understand a new Board ruling – the details can be found in the chapter on Lee Churcher. Gary's sister, Lana, was the first woman in Wales to be licensed as a professional boxer.

Gary Cooper has his hands wrapped by manager Dai Gardiner

Jack Coles, from Tiryberth, lost his chance on the scales. Having won two eliminators, he challenged Welsh lightweight king Warren Kendall in 1947, but turned up more than three pounds overweight. The bout went ahead as a 12-rounder; Coles won the decision, but Kendall kept the title.

Then there was Richie Jenkins, from Griffithstown, who was only 17 when he won for Britain against the US at Wembley Stadium in 1951. Turning pro two years later, he might well have won a Welsh title had he not been barred because he was born in Kent, a rule later relaxed. Jenkins's career ended prematurely when he collapsed in the Ninian Park ring following his first defeat and was left partially paralysed.

Numerous athletes combined boxing with rugby. Jerry Shea was perhaps the best-known, good enough in the ring to draw a Welsh title fight and, between bouts, turning out at full-back for Pill Harriers and Newport. He won four caps for Wales in the years after World War I before going

Lana Cooper, Wales' first licensed woman boxer

north and joining Wigan, also representing his country in the 13-a-side code.

In more modern times, older fans will remember Abertillery fly-half Roddy Crane and Pontypool prop Antonio 'Pedro' Diez, who once produced a perfect one-punch knockout in front of the stand at Pontypool Park, seen by everybody present except the referee. Rhymney plumber Robbie James, big brother of Wales wing Tom, won his first four as a pro only for a shoulder injury to bring his career to a premature end.

Twice-capped fly-half Byron Hayward won a Welsh ABA title in 1994 – son Dylan has done the same at junior level – while back in 1922 Irish international forward Dr WJ Roche was ruled out of the heavyweight competition after injuring a shoulder playing for Newport that afternoon.

Jerry Shea

Newport promoter Jake Channing, who began staging shows in 1927, was a pro runner who also appeared on the wing for Abertillery and Pill Harriers, while winning swimming titles as a schoolboy.

One of the greatest referees of the postwar era was Ike Powell, a former flyweight from Bargoed, who handled more than 1,000 contests across the world, once giving a decision against the legendary Sugar Ray Robinson, while Caerleon teacher Adrian Morgan patrolled the ring for 35 years.

The amateur scene owes much to Monmouthshire men, inside and outside the ropes. When the Welsh ABA was founded, in 1911, the first president was Tom White, from Newport. John Llewellyn, of Fochriw, served as the organisation's chairman for some years until 1964, when he managed the GB boxing team at the Tokyo Olympics. He was also in charge of the successful Wales squad at the 1958 Empire Games in Cardiff, where Newport pair Tom Swadling and Walt Waters made up the training team. Walt's sons, Colin and Glyn, were among five Welsh ABA champions in 1957 from Newport Sporting Club, where Colin took over from his father and coached for 41 years.

Ike Powell, already a ref in his twenties

Alf Ford, from Pontnewynydd, won five Welsh ABA titles in the years leading up to World War

II, and lost on the referee's casting vote to South African J.L. Smith in a middleweight prelim at the 1934 Empire Games.

Aneurin Evans, from Llanbradach, came home from the 1986 event with a silver at super-heavy. But mass withdrawals over apartheid meant he only

boxed in the final, where he was stopped in two rounds by future Hall of Famer Lennox Lewis. The rules were duly changed so that competitors now have to notch at least one victory to get a medal.

Back in the day radio was the only way to follow the big fights and for many years that meant the plummy voice of Newport-born Raymond Glendenning.

Courage is something we take for granted in boxers, but Tredegar bantam Bryn Weed was lauded for a special type of bravery when fire swept through his Hill Street home in 1931. Sadly, despite his efforts, his mother died when she fell while being helped from an upstairs window.

The voice of boxing - Newport-born Raymond Glendenning

Newport welter Jack Blackborow was a useful operator, but brother Perce made bigger headlines when he hid on the *Endeavour* and became part of Sir Ernest Shackleton's 1914 expedition to the Antarctic. When he was discovered, Shackleton told him, "If we run out of food on these trips, we eat the stowaway first." Perce replied, "They'd get a lot more meat off you, sir!"

Ynysddu boxer Cyrus Jones moved to London in the 1920s to seek work. Thirty years later he was a top manager, based in Cricklewood, when his new licence dropped through the letter-box and his dog, Max, chewed it to bits. The Board made him send them the pieces and then charged him two shillings for a replacement!

And just to underline how different things used to be, there is the story of Yuko Sako, from Yokohama, who was actually a small, muscular man from Maesycwmmer with a slightly oriental cast to his features. The recent arrival in the west of jiu-jitsu had generated interest in things Japanese, so booth owner Jack Scarrott painted the guy yellow, cut his hair down to a topknot and gave him his new name. Anything to sell a few tickets!

Monmouthshire was well represented in the 1934 Wales Empire Games team at Wembley. Rear, from left: Alf Ford (Pontnewynydd), Vic Horton (Maindee), Wally Walters and silver medallist Frank Taylor (Risca)
Front: Jackie Pottinger, Albert Barnes, manager Bert Webber and silver medallist J.D. Jones, from Senghenydd.

BIBLIOGRAPHY

The following are among many publications consulted during the writing of this book:

Sporting Life, Mirror of Life, Boxing, Boxing News, Boxing Monthly, Western Mail, South Wales Echo, South Wales Daily News, South Wales Argus, Rhymney Valley Express, Monmouthshire Beacon.

Wales and its Boxers, ed. Peter Stead and Gareth Williams (University of Wales)
No Ordinary Joe, by Joe Calzaghe (Century)
A Fighting Life, by Enzo Calzaghe (Great Northern)
Johnny!, by Alan Roderick (Heron)
King of the Gypsies, by Bartley Gorman (Milo)

The following websites and their contributors were also useful sources of information:

Boxrec.com, Welsh Warriors, www.boxinghistory.org.uk, Amateur Boxing Results, Rootschat, Rootsweb, Ancestry, Find My Past, Gelligaer Historical Society, Newport Past.

ST DAVID'S PRESS

THE BOXERS OF WALES

CARDIFF

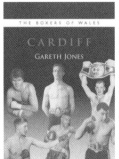

'Some of the greatest boxers in Britain have come out of Cardiff and this book is a must read for fight fans, whether you're Welsh or not.'*Colin Hart, The Sun*

'This book is not just about the famous fighters, it's about the forgotten heroes.'
Steve Bunce, Boxing Broadcaster & Journalist

'A compelling and fascinating study.'   *Claude Abrams, Editor, Boxing News*

'Boxing fans in and out of Wales will love this collection of mini biographies profiling no less than 50 classic boxers from the Cardiff area...An indispensable guide to Cardiff boxers and a great resource for compiling those pub quizzes!'
South Wales Argus

'...a long overdue reminder of how much Cardiff has given to boxing. The verdict? A knockout.'   *Dan O'Neill, South Wales Echo*

978-1-902719-26-9 160pp £14.99 PB

THE BOXERS OF WALES

MERTHYR

ABERDARE & PONTYPRIDD

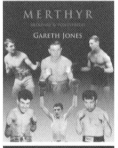

'masterpiece... a must-read for any boxing fan...Compelling stuff.'
Steve Lillis, News of the World

'The Valleys of South Wales have produced many fighters known worldwide ... but this book reminds us that there were others who lit up the ring in their day.'   *Gareth A. Davies, Daily Telegraph*

'For generations of Merthyr's youth, boxing has been as much a means of self-expression as a way out of grinding poverty. This book does full justice to a sporting tradition that has shaped the town's character and given the world some unforgettable champions.'   *Mario Basini, Author, 'Real Merthyr'*

978-1-902719-29-0 160pp £14.99 PB

THE BOXERS OF WALES

RHONDDA

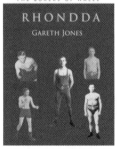

'When Boxing News marked its centenary in 2009 by choosing the best British boxer of the previous 100 years, we opted for the one and only Jimmy Wilde. But the Rhondda produced many other outstanding fighters, as this book reminds us.'   *Tris Dixon, Editor, Boxing News*

'When it comes to in-depth research, they don't come much better than Gareth Jones – as his latest tome perfectly illustrates, with a trawl through the Rhondda's staggering boxing history. The likes of the great Tommy Farr and Jimmy Wilde get the Jones treatment, along with a host of tales surrounding so many boxers from this mining area that produced such a rich seam of boxing greats.'
Kevin Francis, Boxing Correspondent, Daily Star

978-1-902719-33-7 160pp £14.99 PB

THE BOXERS OF WALES

SWANSEA & LLANELLI

'My co-commentator, Enzo Maccarinelli, keeps telling me what a great fight town Swansea is. And here's the evidence. It's not just about the big names, like Colin Jones, Ronnie James and the Curvises – here you can learn of the only Welsh-speaker ever to win a Scottish title and the Llanelli girl who took on Germany's boxing queen. A great read!'
John Rawling, Commentator, BoxNation

'Wales has a rich boxing history and there is no one better than Gareth Jones at bringing vividly to life the exploits of the many fine Welsh fighters, from the famous to the largely forgotten. This book is a must for all serious boxing fans.'   *Graham Houston, Editor, Boxing Monthly*

978-1-902719-450 176pp £14.99 PB